KIND SIR

KIND SIR

A COMEDY IN THREE ACTS

by

NORMAN KRASNA

DRAMATISTS PLAY SERVICE, INC.
New York

For Bob Ross

KIND SIR was first presented by Joshua Logan at the Alvin Theatre, New York City, on November 4, 1953. It was directed by Mr. Logan, with settings and lighting by Jo Mielziner and costumes by Main Bocher. Marshall Jamison was associate producer and director. The cast was as follows:

Cast

ANNIE MILLER..........................Margalo Gillmore
MARGARET MUNSON......................Dorothy Stickney
JANE KIMBALL..............................Mary Martin
ALFRED MUNSON...........................Frank Conroy
PHILIP CLAIR.............................Charles Boyer
CARL MILLER...............................Robert Ross

SYNOPSIS OF SCENES

The action takes place in the New York apartment of Miss Jane Kimball.

ACT I

Scene 1. Early Fall. Six P.M.
Scene 2. One A.M.

ACT II

Scene 1. Two weeks later.
Scene 2. Six months later.

ACT III

Scene 1. Five hours later.
Scene 2. The following evening. Before midnight.

ACT ONE

ACT ONE

Scene One

*The curtain rises on a charming and expensive New York
residential hotel suite. A piano, Right; a sewing arrangement,
lamp and basket, near a wing chair, Left; a butler's tray bar,
Rear, Left; and the usual sofa, coffee table, Forward Leftish;
and game table and three chairs, Forward, Rightish; make up
the basic pieces. Behind the sofa is another table; on it, a
telephone.*

*In the Rear wall is a vestibule slightly raised above the rest
of the room. Two doors lead off this vestibule, the Right door
leading to the pantry and maid's room, and the Left door to
the hallway, which is the outside entrance. Upstage in the
Right wall is a door leading to the master bedroom; Upstage
in the Left wall is a door to the guest room.*

*The stage is deserted. Annie enters from the pantry. Annie is
forty-five, Jane's maid and companion, all wise, all knowing.
She carries a vase of flowers which she places on a table, and
surveys them. She would start back, but the hallway door
opens, admitting Margaret, key in hand. Margaret Munson
is the wife of the Assistant Secretary of State, Jane's sister, two
years older, funny and nice. She is in evening clothes and is
carrying a small overnight bag.*

ANNIE

Good evening, Mrs. Munson.

11

MARGARET

(*Surprised*) Annie! What are you doing here?

ANNIE

We flew home this morning.

MARGARET

What for? Rehearsing a new play?

ANNIE

No. Miss Kimball just got bored with Bermuda.

MARGARET

(*A sigh. She walks toward the master bedroom Down Right*) Jane!

ANNIE

She's in the park, feeding the squirrels.

MARGARET

Couldn't she find any squirrels in Bermuda? Annie, Mister Munson is coming in from Washington and dressing here in the guest room.

ANNIE

(*Taking the bag*) I'll unpack his things.

MARGARET

Thank you. (*Annie goes into the guest room with the bag. Margaret takes off her wrap and wanders to the piano. She studies a picture of Jane, and shakes her head. She sits at the piano and does the scale, applying herself. The hall door opens and Jane Kimball enters. Jane may not be the First Lady of the Theatre, but she's in the first half dozen. Thirty fiveish, beautiful and endearing.*)

JANE

Hello, Sis!

MARGARET

Jane! (*They embrace*)

JANE

How are you?

MARGARET

Fine.

JANE

And Alfred?

MARGARET

Fine.

JANE

And the family?

MARGARET

Fine. Enough of that, eh?

JANE

Fine!

MARGARET

What's wrong with you, Jane? You plan to be away for a month and you're back in ten days.

JANE

(*Taking off her coat*) I didn't find it interesting.

MARGARET

Is it possible the trouble isn't with Bermuda?

JANE

Possible.

MARGARET

What happened to that British colonel you mentioned in your letter? The one that looked like Anthony Eden?

JANE

He didn't talk like Anthony Eden. I don't think he knew more than a dozen words. 'Scotch and soda,' and one or two more.

MARGARET

You were impressed with him when you met him.

JANE

I hadn't heard the dozen words.

MARGARET

What is it you expect of a man? There's a limit to how entertaining they are.

JANE

They ought to be able to talk a little. Simple sentences.

MARGARET

You said he was good looking and danced beautifully. That's all a woman is entitled to. You can always read a good book!

JANE

Dear little sister. Go wash your mind with soap.

MARGARET

I'm not your little sister. I'm the older.

JANE

This is a side of you I've never seen before. Sort of a maternal white slaver.

MARGARET

You're developing a new side of your own. Sort of a crotchety old maid!

JANE

(*Stung*) Any other subject?

MARGARET

(*Hastily repentant*) I'm sorry, darling. That didn't come out the way I meant it. You're hardly a crotchety old maid.

JANE

What am I?

MARGARET

You're a famous, beautiful, talented woman who's the envy of everyone who knows you.

JANE

(*Wryly*) Then they don't know me.

MARGARET

Jane, don't stay in this mood.

JANE

You don't select moods, sister dear. They select you.

MARGARET

Why don't you marry David Wilson?

JANE

Because I don't love him.

MARGARET

Why not?

JANE

I don't know why not. I try to love him. I just don't.

MARGARET

Someone'll come along.

JANE

When?

MARGARET

Soon.

JANE

It's later than you think. And the field's getting smaller. Not many men have the ego for marrying—(*Sarcasm*) famous women! (*A forced smile*) I'm beginning to think it's against nature!

MARGARET

Nonsense! (*To change the subject*) Where are you having dinner?

JANE

I'm not. I had something late.

MARGARET

Come along with us. You'll feel better in a girdle.

JANE

Where are you going?

MARGARET

To the Waldorf.

JANE

For dinner?

MARGARET

Certainly, they serve food. (*Jane looks at her*) It's a banquet.

JANE

That's what I thought.

MARGARET

Sometimes the speaker is very interesting.

JANE

I remember the last one. The Dutch Ambassador spoke for an hour and fifteen minutes. In Dutch. (*Annie crosses from the guest bedroom to Rear, Right, taking Jane's coat, gloves and bag*)

MARGARET

We'll go someplace later.

JANE

Wild horses.

MARGARET

Jane, you're going to have to make some effort to get out of this—(*She's stuck*) this morass of lethargy.

JANE

It's my morass of lethargy and I love it.

MARGARET

Are you going to do a new play?

JANE

That reminds me! I've got to call Lew! (*She goes to phone*) Molly, may I have Madison seven two three hundred. . . . I had a very nice time, Molly, thank you. (*She waits. Then in a British accent*) Is this the Yaeger Theatrical Agency? Bermuda calling Mister Yaeger. I'll hold on. . . . Mister Yaeger? . . . one moment, please, Bermuda calling. (*Her own voice, raised for long distance*) Hello, Lew—Jane! . . . Fine, fine, never better. . . . I did check out of the hotel, but I've moved in with friends. . . . Weather's beautiful, how is it in New York? . . . Is that so? . . . (*Margaret enjoys this subterfuge*) . . . Well, I haven't made up my mind yet. I like the play, Lew, I just don't know if I'm going to do anything this year. . . . Well, I'll tell them something definite this week. That's a promise. (*Through the hall door comes Alfred Munson, husband of Margaret, the Assistant Secretary of State. He is fifty five, bright, pleasant, imposing. He is in business clothes*)

ALFRED

Jane! This is a surprise! (*Jane claps her hand over the phone and Margaret wigwags violently*)

MARGARET

Ssh!

JANE

Well, let's leave it at that, Lew. . . . No, don't call me here, I'll call you. Goodbye, Lew. . . . (*Other voice*) Bermuda operator. Is that all? Are you through, madam? Thank you. (*She hangs up*)

ALFRED

(*Mystified*) What's that for?

JANE

(*Rising*) I'm in Bermuda.

ALFRED

When did you get back?

JANE

This morning. (*They embrace warmly*) How's Washington?

ALFRED

Washington! (*He kisses her, and turns to Margaret*) And how are you, dear?

MARGARET

Fine, Alfred.

ALFRED

How's everything at home?

MARGARET

Fine. (*Back to Jane*) Come on, I'll help you dress. You're only feeling sorry for yourself.

JANE

Not at all. I'm feeling sorry for you!

MARGARET

She's coming along with us.

ALFRED

Good!

JANE

She is not!

ALFRED

You're more than welcome, Jane.

JANE

The Dutch Ambassador. I think of him often.

MARGARET

I told you he's not going to be there! (*To Alfred*) Is he?

ALFRED

Oh, no! That was an official state dinner. This one's going to be quite interesting.

MARGARET

(*To Jane*) See? There you are!

JANE

(*Suspicious*) Who's it for?

ALFRED .

It's for the hard currency countries. There are going to be a number of speakers, who'll—(*He's stuck*) well—speak.

JANE

On hard currency?

ALFRED

Yes.

JANE

The Dutch Ambassador is growing on me.

ALFRED

It isn't as bad as it sounds—

JANE

I go no place where they don't speak Dutch!

MARGARET

Alfred, it might be better if I stayed here and kept Jane company. She's depressed.

JANE

I am not!

MARGARET

You are so!

ALFRED

You'll do nothing of the sort! You're coming along with me! There are place cards!

MARGARET

(*Eyeing Alfred*) When I think that I could have married a man in woolen goods!

ALFRED

Well, you're lucky you didn't. We're lowering the import tax on woolens! That's off the record. (*From the hall entrance, Philip Clair appears. He is fortyish, handsome, striking. The big point is, he and Jane complement each other so perfectly that it is apparent immediately. At the moment he stands there, his bag in hand*)

PHILIP

Excuse me. The door was open.

ALFRED

Where were you? I looked all through the train!

PHILIP

I had some last minute appointments. I took the plane. (*There is a pause. Jane and Philip are so aware of each other it is almost embarrassing*)

ALFRED

May I present Mister Philip Clair. Mrs. Munson.

MARGARET

How do you do.

PHILIP

How do you do.

ALFRED

And my sister-in-law, Miss Jane Kimball.

JANE

How do you do.

PHILIP

How do you do. Miss Kimball is no stranger to me. I've seen you often on the stage. And I'm a fervent admirer.

JANE

Why, thank you, kind sir.

PHILIP

I once stayed over an extra day, in Cleveland, because you were billed to appear, and then the performance was cancelled.

JANE

I am sorry.

PHILIP

It turned out to be a fortunate delay. I made a good deal of money by it.

JANE

I'm glad.

PHILIP

(*Exaggerated gallantry*) I'd have been happy to trade the money for the performance.

JANE

Well! Would you be interested in the performance now? I'll play all the parts. How much money was it? (*They keep looking at each other*)

ALFRED

I asked Philip to come up here and change his clothes. He's in from Washington just for the dinner. I had no idea you'd be back, Jane.

JANE

That's perfectly all right.

PHILIP

It's no trouble for me to go to a hotel.

JANE

You're more than welcome.

PHILIP

It's an imposition—

JANE

I owe you something for Cleveland. (*He smiles. None of it is lost on Margaret. A pause*)

MARGARET

Where is Mrs. Clair going to dress?

PHILIP

There is no Mrs. Clair. (*A pause*)

MARGARET

Now do we have to go to the silly dinner? The speaker'll bore us to death. Nobody'd miss us.

ALFRED

They'd miss him, my dear. He's the speaker. (*A moment's embarrassment*)

MARGARET

(*To Philip, matter-of-factly*) This happens to me all the time. I once asked the butler at the French Embassy if he cared to waltz. He waltzed beautifully.

PHILIP

(*Smiles*) You're right about the speech being dull. I've heard it.

ALFRED

Of course, we could go some place afterwards?

PHILIP

It's the only hope for the evening.

ALFRED

What do you say, Jane?

JANE

Oh no, I couldn't.

MARGARET

Why not?

JANE

For one thing, I'm not dressed—

MARGARET

Neither are they. We'll race them.

JANE

We wouldn't come out even.

MARGARET

It doesn't matter if we're late, we have the man with the speech! They can't start until he comes! (*To them*) She has to be coaxed! (*To Philip*) You coax her!

PHILIP

I'm an extra man and you'd make the dinner come out even.

JANE

How many people are going to be there?

PHILIP

(*Smiling*) Six hundred.

JANE

(*Getting up*) Yes. Five hundred and ninety-nine people in a room does look untidy. That's all I wanted, an intelligent reason. (*She goes to master bedroom, indicating for Philip where he is to change, Left*) Last one dressed is last. (*Philip takes his bag and exits Left, to the guest room. Alfred goes to the phone. Margaret has watched Philip's every move*)

ALFRED

(*Into phone*) Plaza 6-9200.

MARGARET

(*Meaning Philip*) Who—for heaven's sakes—is that?

ALFRED

Stop breathing so hard.

MARGARET

I didn't know it was showing. Who and what is he and speak slowly.

ALFRED

He's a very bright gentleman we're trying to get into the State Department. And we're not having much luck. (*Into phone*) Harris? This is Mister Munson. One more at our table. A place card for 'Miss Jane Kimball'. . . . Next to Mister Clair . . . Fine. (*He hangs up*)

MARGARET

What about Mister Clair?

ALFRED

What would you like to know?

MARGARET

Everything! And I mean everything.

ALFRED

Well, I don't think he's romantically attached, which is what you're hinting.

MARGARET

I'm not hinting! How do you know he isn't attached?

ALFRED

We've had dinner together and he's been alone.

MARGARET

So were you. I assume.

ALFRED

That's right. I don't know what he does after he leaves me. I'll follow him next time.

MARGARET

Of course he hasn't any money?

ALFRED

(*Amused*) You notice we're giving a dinner about money and he's the speaker. He's a very rich man.

MARGARET

There's something the matter with his health?

ALFRED

Hardly. He beat our club squash champion six straight games. You have to be pretty healthy for that.

MARGARET

There's a catch someplace. He's still in love with his grandmother. Or he knits. He couldn't have gotten this far otherwise.

ALFRED

What I'd like you to do, dear, is give Mr. Clair your hostess rush. He doesn't know many people in the East. If we can make him happy here it might just decide him.

MARGARET

(*Determinedly*) Oh, I'll make him happy! I'll make him happy if I have to tie him down!

ALFRED

We're anxious to get him. There aren't many like him available as public servants.

MARGARET

I'm not thinking of the public. My poor spinster sister.

ALFRED

(*Smiling*) Say, you never can tell. He seems like a very nice sort.

MARGARET

(*Now seriously*) Alfred, I'm afraid to let myself think of it. It would be heaven sent.

ALFRED

Well, let's keep our fingers crossed. Dress her up pretty.

MARGARET

Don't let him get out the window. (*They smile at each other. She goes Right to master bedroom. He goes Left to guest room.*)

CURTAIN

ACT ONE

Scene Two

One A.M. Carl Miller, Annie's husband, is turning on the sewing lamp. He is fifty five, gentle, and timid. Annie enters from Rear, Right. She has a very uneven skirt wrapped around her, which she has evidently basted herself, and she carries a sewing basket and yardstick.

ANNIE

I can't make the hem come out even. (*She models for him*) It pulls in the front and drags in the back. I tried everything.

CARL

(*Smiling at her effort*) You have no talent with the needle, Annie.

ANNIE

It's not woman's work.

CARL

True, my dear wife, true. (*He will work on the skirt, on Annie*)

ANNIE

(*Looking at her watch*) She's out so late, she must be having a wonderful time. I'm so glad.

CARL

Miss Kimball used this color last year.

29

ANNIE

In the second act. It's a good color for her.

CARL

What about this year? I don't see anything announced in the papers.

ANNIE

I don't know. They send her plays, she sends them back. She's got one now she likes a little.

CARL

It's getting late in the season.

ANNIE

She doesn't seem to care like she used to. We forget, she's been a star a long time. The novelty's gone.

CARL

It's never gone. Once you have the theatre in your blood you can never leave it. Look at me.

ANNIE

You? You're a tailor!

CARL

I'm a wardrobe man. If I wanted to be called a tailor I could get more money.

ANNIE

Couldn't you be a tailor and think of yourself as a wardrobe man?

CARL

No. The theatre's in my blood.

ANNIE

(*Deprecating*) Ah ha. (*She gives Carl the skirt*)

CARL

Don't you believe there's such a thing?

ANNIE

As soon as they show it to me under a microscope I'll believe it.

CARL

Irving Berlin said it in a song, 'There's no business like show business!'

ANNIE

And a lucky thing, too.

CARL

You were an actress. When you decided to retire I notice you still associated yourself with the theatre. Why was that?

ANNIE

In the first place, I didn't decide to retire. Nobody hired me. In the second place, what did I play on the stage? I played maids! That's all anybody wanted me for, to be a maid. Altogether I played fifteen maids! Well, that's what I'm playing now. My sixteenth maid. But this part's a good one. Not 'Yes madam, no madam, will you have coffee served in the drawing room?' This is a big, fat part! It runs a whole day long! And what a performance I'm giving! Superb! You can put all the critics in one room, and they can look at me all day with magnifying glasses, and not one of them can tell me from a real maid. That's my idea of acting!

CARL

It's not the same. There's a difference.

ANNIE

The difference is no stage manager is pinching me!

CARL

That trouble I haven't got. I'm a wardrobe man.

ANNIE

You're a tailor! You're just working for less money! (*The sound of voices off scene Rear Left is heard. Jane, Philip, Margaret and Alfred appear from hallway, all in evening dress*)

JANE

(*In very good spirits*) Hello, Mister Miller.

CARL

(*Half standing, with the skirt and workbasket in his lap*) Good evening, Miss Kimball.

ANNIE

Carl is fixing your hem. He helps me with my sewing.

JANE

Well, good for you. And good for me, too.

CARL

It's nothing.

ANNIE

Come, Carl.

CARL

Good night, Miss Kimball.

JANE

Good night, Mister Miller.

ANNIE

Good night, Mrs. Munson. Mister Munson.

ALFRED

Good night.

MARGARET

Good night, Annie.

ANNIE

I'll bring some ice. (*And she's out, Right, Rear, preceded by Carl*)

JANE

(*Happily*) Well! (*She looks at her guests*)

MARGARET

(*Sitting*) Scotch and water. Until the ice comes.

PHILIP

(*As Jane goes toward the liquor tray*) Can I help?

JANE

It's no trouble. Alfred?

ALFRED

(*Looking at his watch*) I'm afraid we haven't time for a drink. Our train leaves in twenty-five minutes.

MARGARET

Oh no!

ALFRED

Oh yes! I'll get my bag and we'll run along.

MARGARET

We're only ten minutes away.

ALFRED

Well, cross town and all.

JANE

(*Stopping, disappointed*) Oh.

PHILIP

(*Going too*) Excuse me. (*Both men are out, Left, to guest room*)

MARGARET

(*Frustrated*) I'd miss the train, but the next one's not for two hours!

JANE

Don't be ridiculous.

MARGARET

I'm going to invite him to dinner for Friday! I ought to do it by mail but I can't take a chance!

JANE

Now don't overdo it. You're going to be a little obvious.

MARGARET

Listen, we have to work fast! We've got our hands on him now only because those women in Washington haven't seen him yet. When they do we'll be trampled in the rush!

JANE

Let's not worry about that.

MARGARET

(*Close to her*) Now don't tell me you don't like him! This one talks and everything!

JANE

(*Conceding*) Oh, he's all right. He's interesting.

MARGARET

Interesting! (*She raises her right hand*) Twenty years married. Never once! And I've a confession to make. At dinner I thought he was pressing his knee against mine. It turned out to be the table leg! I was disappointed!

JANE

You're a big talker.

MARGARET

If he plays his cards right I'll be a big doer. (*The two men come back, with their bags*)

ALFRED

Well, we're off.

JANE

(*Offering her hand*) Good night, Mister Clair. I had a very nice evening.

PHILIP

The obligation's all mine. I don't remember ever having a better time.

JANE

And I enjoyed your speech very much. I'm crazy about hard currency.

MARGARET

Well, I wasn't clear about some of it. Can you come to dinner and explain it again? Friday night?

PHILIP

I'd be delighted.

MARGARET

What about you, Jane? Are you free?

JANE

Friday night? (*She's thinking*) This Friday?

MARGARET

(*Eyeing her*) Yes, dear, this Friday.

JANE

Let me think. I have something. It's only tentative—

MARGARET

Can't you get out of it?

JANE

(*Impulsively*) Yes, I can!

MARGARET

Good! (*To Philip*) We live in Rye, you know. You and Alfred can come in right from Washington.

PHILIP

Can't we arrange this on the way to the station?

MARGARET

(*A thought*) Why, you're not with us! We're going to Rye, you're going to Washington. What time does your train leave?

PHILIP

Not for an hour.

MARGARET

You don't mean to sit in the station all that time?

PHILIP

I don't mind. Really, I don't. I have some magazines. (*There is quite a pause*)

MARGARET

Well, that's ridiculous. (*Another small pause*) Wouldn't it be all right if you kept the door open?

PHILIP

(*He smiles*) Well—

JANE

(*Finally*) Yes, we could do that. You can read your magazines right here.

PHILIP

I'd be keeping you up.

JANE

I'm not a bit sleepy.

MARGARET

(*Taking Alfred*) Come, dear. We mustn't miss our train.

ALFRED

Yah! (*His hand out*) I'm not going to press you further. No matter how you decide, we're all very obligated to you for the job you *have* done. The Secretary particularly asked me to tell you that.

PHILIP

I'm very flattered, and it was an honor to be asked.

MARGARET

Good night, Mister Clair.

PHILIP

Good night, Mr. Munson.

MARGARET

Jane.

JANE

'Night.

ALFRED

Good night, Jane.

JANE

Good night, Alfred. (*They leave thru hall door, Margaret throwing Jane a meaning look. The door is heard closing, loud*) They seem to have forgotten.

PHILIP

Yes, they have. (*Annie comes in Rear, Right, with a bucket of ice. She is surprised at seeing just two. Jane looks enquiringly at him*) Bourbon and water. (*Annie leaves Rear, Right looking at Philip, delighted*)

JANE

Well, anyway, Annie'll keep *her* door open. (*The door slams shut. Jane busies herself with the liquor*) How thick a drink do you like?

PHILIP

Oh, a finger and a half. I'm not much for after dinner. (*He notices*) Aren't you having one?

JANE

(*Bringing him the drink*) I don't think so. But you do. I like to see a man with a glass in his hand. It's becoming.

PHILIP

I'll gladly hold it.

JANE

(*She sits. He does, too*) No, you have to sip it once in a while, too. That's part of the picture.

PHILIP

Shouldn't you be holding a cigarette?

JANE

Why?

PHILIP

You always are—on the back pages of the magazines.

JANE

Oh, I don't smoke. They pay me. And they still send me car-
tons of cigarettes every month. They sent them all during the
war. My friends were crazy about me. The smoking ones.

PHILIP

I wish I'd known you. I had an awful time.

JANE

Well, you leave your name, and if there's another war— (*She
doesn't like the remark*) That's awful callous, isn't it?

PHILIP

It's an attitude we've all fallen into.

JANE

Do you think there'll be another?

PHILIP

War? (*He shrugs*) I pray, like everyone else.

JANE

Where were you the last one?

PHILIP

Nothing dramatic. At a desk in the Federal Reserve.

JANE

I'm sure it was something somebody had to do.

PHILIP

Yes, I kept saying that. I've been saying it recently too. I've been offered a job in the State Department.

JANE

An interesting job?

PHILIP

Well, they're not asking me to be Ambassador to the Court of St. James. It's to do the same banking work I've always done, that I thought I'd retired from.

JANE

When did you retire?

PHILIP

Three years ago.

JANE

You're very fortunate.

PHILIP

I guess so. (*Second thought*) Yes, I am.

JANE

Are you going to take the job in the State Department?

PHILIP

I don't know. I probably should. Public service and all that. But it's damn dull.

JANE

What would you do otherwise?

PHILIP

You hit on it. That's damn dull too. Too many damns for you?

JANE

No, no, I've heard the word mentioned.

PHILIP

Well, it turns out doing nothing is damn dull too. I've been to Europe half a dozen times the last three years. I keep clothes at the George Cinq and Claridges. (*It occurs to him*) Sounds affected doesn't it?

JANE

Not at all. Very dashing and glamorous.

PHILIP

They're only business suits. I've been thinking about spending the winter in Mexico. Have you ever been there?

JANE

No, I haven't.

PHILIP

But that doesn't seem too appetizing either. There's supposed to be an uncomfortable two weeks until you get used to the water.

JANE

I've heard that. Couldn't you try the State Department job? Just for a while, to see if you liked it?

PHILIP

Once you take it you're obligated to stay a while. It's policy.
I can understand that.

JANE

I see.

PHILIP

Any advice?

JANE

Well, if you go to Mexico, drink bottled water.

PHILIP

I'll do that.

JANE

I understand where people slip up is in brushing their teeth.
Bottled water there, too.

PHILIP

I'd never have thought of it. Seems like an awful lot of
trouble.

JANE

Yes, it does. Take the job in the State Department. Brush your
teeth with anything.

PHILIP

Say, that might decide me.

JANE

Have you ever lived in Washington any length of time?

PHILIP

No, I haven't.

JANE

There's an interesting social life once you adjust yourself to it.
Being single you'll be in great demand. There's quite a short-
age. And, of course, you can spend week-ends in New York.

PHILIP

I've never had a real wonderful time in New York.

JANE

How dare you, sir?

PHILIP

I didn't mean to be disrespectful. I'm sure it's my fault.

JANE

(*Maintaining the burlesque*) May I enquire where you're from?

PHILIP

San Francisco.

JANE

I've been there. Charming village.

PHILIP

Oh, you're bigger, there's no denying that.

JANE

I speak of cultural pursuits. Our theatre, our opera, our museums—

PHILIP

When were you in a museum last?

JANE

I go daily.

PHILIP

Oh, well, then! We're not as isolated out there as you imagine. The stage coach makes it pretty regularly now. We get the New York shows. Not the same year, but eventually. We have opera. Not much, but enough.

JANE

I take it you are not an opera lover?

PHILIP

I admire it, but it escapes me. We have a whole ballet season.
That doesn't escape me.

JANE

You like the ballet?

PHILIP

I do indeed. Very much. (*There is a pause*)

JANE

Would you care to go Saturday night? I have regular seats.
(*A pause. She is terribly conscious of having made such a
definite lead, and the pause is accentuating it*)

PHILIP

I'm a married man, Miss Kimball. (*She looks at him a second,
hiding the disappointment she feels, and then, her sense of
humor rescuing her, she laughs. He does, too*) I'm sorry. (*She
still laughs*) I'm awfully sorry.

JANE

(*Still laughing*) That was perfectly all right.

PHILIP

When I first came in, I said there was no Mrs. Clair. I meant
no Mrs. Clair dressing. I've been conscious of it all evening.

JANE

(*Smiling*) Yes, I would say you've been palming yourself off as
a single man.

PHILIP

I must have sounded like an idiot, blurting it out.

JANE

No, not at all. It was very proper, and pertinent.

PHILIP

And rather vain, too.

JANE

Vain? Why?

PHILIP

The implication was you wouldn't be able to keep your hands off me.

JANE

Well, you'll never know now.

PHILIP

(*Smiles*) I have a suspicion.

JANE

(*Different tone*) If you felt that why did you have to warn me?

PHILIP

(*Matching it*) Those are the rules, between grown men and women. Or should be. The game is so one-sided, for a man.

JANE

Yes, I think it is, too. Well, you are a rarity.

PHILIP

I don't believe I am.

JANE

Oh, you are, you are. I speak from vast experience. Men usually don't mention they're married at all. Or if it's something you know, they explain they're either misunderstood, or separated and can't possibly get a divorce. The last is the most popular this year. Where is Mrs. Clair? In Washington?

PHILIP

San Francisco.

JANE

I see.

PHILIP

I'm afraid this changes my status here. Morally.

JANE

You're not compromising me, if that's what's bothering you. You'd have to spend the night. The law is quite clear on it. Ipso facto if you spend the night. I was in a play that had that in it.

PHILIP

It doesn't seem fair to the woman. I hope there are loopholes.

JANE

You have a well developed sense of chivalry. You're a throwback to King Arthur and his knights of the Round Table. I mean it as a compliment.

PHILIP

I'll take it as a compliment. (*There is the bong bong of church chimes striking two*)

JANE

Two o'clock at St. Timothy's. (*She gets up. He does, too*) I've had a most enjoyable evening.

PHILIP

So have I. (*He gets his bag*) I hope this doesn't affect the dinner at your sister's home. We'll be quite chaperoned.

JANE

Of course not.

PHILIP

(*He looks at her a moment*) I hope your vanity isn't hurt. I've been sorely tempted to forget the rules. I've been debating it all evening.

JANE

(*She smiles*) Evidently your honor is stronger than my beauty.

PHILIP

(*Strong*) You see, I am separated from my wife, and I can't possibly get a divorce! The same line all the other boys are pulling this year! How the hell was I going to say it? (*Jane looks at him, anew*)

JANE

Oh!

PHILIP

I can't help if they're using it so much. There's no copyright on it!

JANE

I see.

PHILIP

So—good night! (*He walks toward the hall door. He turns at the entrance. Soft again*) And thank you again. Thank you very much. (*There is a moment. The decision to make is quite clear. The moment is right now*)

JANE

Good seats to the ballet are quite hard to get. Would you like to come?

PHILIP

(*Fervently*) I'd like nothing better in the whole world.

JANE

Good night.

PHILIP

Good night. (*He's out. She doesn't know whether she's done the right thing. She's flushed, surprised at her own impulsiveness. She starts to turn the lamps out. After the first one, the phone rings. She goes to it*)

JANE

Hello? . . . Hello, Lew . . . Certainly I'm in New York . . . Oh! . . . Well, I pretended I was calling you from Bermuda . . . I just wanted to hide . . . Oh, no! Where did they see me? . . . How much did you bet them? . . . Oh no! . . . Lew, such language! . . . Well, maybe I'll make it up to you. I think I'll do the play, Lew . . . I'll make up my mind definitely over the week-end . . . Yes, it might be a nice season. Good night, Lew. (*She hangs up. Smiling, she puts out the remaining lamp. She hums, a mixture of apprehension and happiness. She goes into her bedroom as the Curtain comes down*)

CURTAIN

ACT TWO

ACT TWO

Scene One

Scene: the same. Two weeks later. Four bowls of yellow roses have been added to the room. Six o'clock. Jane, carefully dressed, comes from the pantry carrying a vase, followed by Annie, who is carrying a play script.

JANE

(*Rather sing song*) I'm very fond of you, you know. I think I'm fonder of you than anyone else.

ANNIE

I'm fond of you, too. (*Jane puts the vase down, comparing it with the one there*)

JANE

We always did have a good time together.

ANNIE

Yes, we did. (*Jane has decided to take the flowers out of one vase and put them in the other*)

JANE

Then why did we quarrel so much?

ANNIE

It's our natures, darling.

51

JANE

Arthur, could it be we were just bad mannered?

ANNIE

No, Sybil.

JANE

(*Different voice, still concentrating on the flowers*) No, Sybil, no Sybil—

ANNIE

(*Prompting*) In any case—

JANE

In any case, this is the end of our road. How strange that we can part so casually, with just a handshake, as men do. (*Her natural voice*) They're beautiful roses.

ANNIE

There's another boxful in the pantry. We've run out of vases.

JANE

Get some more!

ANNIE

Don't you think he'll taper off?

JANE

I hope not!

ANNIE

Well, he's been sending them for two weeks now. Maybe he won't. (*Gesturing with the script*) Come on, now.

JANE

(*Memorizing voice*) Darling, I'll miss you terribly. I'll walk into a crowded room and someone will be standing the way

you stand. He'll hold his head the way you hold your head.
The way you hold your knife and fork.

ANNIE

I don't hold my knife and fork any special way.

JANE

Why, you hold your fork straight up, as a little boy does. You
do, Arthur! (*The buzzer rings off Rear, Left. Looking at her
watch*) Oh my! (*Annie grabs the emptied vase, and runs to
the pantry. Jane fixes her hair, surveys her dress. As Annie
crosses from the pantry to Left, Jane strikes a pose she hopes is
effective. It doesn't suit her. She seems to be having trouble
with her hands. In a last second decision she dives for a magazine and sits on the couch. Annie and Philip appear from hall
door*)

ANNIE

Mister Clair.

JANE

(*Courteous, friendly, nothing more*) Hello. You're very prompt.

PHILIP

You said six.

JANE

I meant six.

PHILIP

I used to work in a bank. Some of it's hung on.

JANE

Thank you for the beautiful roses.

PHILIP

You're quite welcome.

JANE

You're sending too many, too often. The buds aren't fully opened before new ones arrive. That's wasting.

PHILIP

I'm partial to yellow roses. (*Annie waits*)

JANE

Would you like a cocktail?

PHILIP

No, thanks.

JANE

Nothing, Annie. (*Annie goes Rear, Right. They wait for her to go. He steps to her. He takes her by the shoulders and kisses her. It's a tender kiss, not possessive. No matter what you suspect their relationship has been, they have yet to know each other very well, or fall in love*)

PHILIP

You're looking lovely.

JANE

It's just this light.

PHILIP

Yes, it is. Shining inside out.

JANE

Good! Something from the bank?

PHILIP

It might be my conscience but I think Annie is smirking at me.

JANE

Probably.

PHILIP

We're not fooling her?

JANE

I don't think so.

PHILIP

I'm very circumspect in front of her.

JANE

(*Smiles*) Too circumspect. You're overdoing it.

PHILIP

(*He nods*) I'll try to strike a better balance. I hope you're hungry.

JANE

(*She nods*) Hmm.

PHILIP

Can we go back to the Italian place?

JANE

Let's.

PHILIP

I was afraid you'd be tired of it.

JANE

Oh, no!

PHILIP

I'm going to order the same thing I had before.

JANE

So am I. Let's do everything we did last week-end.

PHILIP

(*Deliberately*) Exactly.

JANE

What did you do all week?

PHILIP

I called you every day!

JANE

What did you do last night?

PHILIP

(*Impressed*) Now that's odd. I did do something. I've been meaning to make a lot of it. Am I that transparent?

JANE

No. Womanly intuition.

PHILIP

It's frightening. Well, are you ready to be impressed?

JANE

Fire away.

PHILIP

I had dinner with the President.

JANE

My!

PHILIP

My indeed!

JANE

What did you have to eat?

PHILIP

Lamb chops.

JANE

(*Disappointed*) Oh, no!

PHILIP

What did you expect?

JANE

Something more pretentious, befitting the occasion.

PHILIP

Well, it wasn't an occasion for him. He eats every night.

JANE

How did you come to be invited?

PHILIP

I— (*He's hesitant*) well—you see—

JANE

What is it?

PHILIP

I decided yesterday to take the job in the State Department.

JANE

(*Sincerely*) Good.

PHILIP

I made my mind up after I spoke to you.

JANE

(*She is pleased and touched*) I'm very flattered.

PHILIP

Well, I told Alfred, and he went in and told the Secretary, and about half an hour after that the phone rang, and someone said, "The White House." I thought for a minute it was a joke—some of the fellows do things like that—and I said, "Yes?" and a voice said, "How about pot luck tonight." Well, it sounded like the President's voice but I was still suspicious, I didn't want to be taken in, and I guess I was a little nervous, too, and I said, "Well, I'm not sure—," and he said, "Oh come on now, it's as good a meal as you can get in town. You be here!" and I said, "Yes, sir," and he hung up. That was all.

JANE

(*Touched*) That was very nice. Well, tell me everything that happened.

PHILIP

Small talk, really.

JANE

You must have discussed something!

PHILIP

Let's see. (*Thinking*) Is it worth while taking saccharine in your coffee instead of sugar? That took most of the time. The President said it wasn't.

JANE

He's wrong.

PHILIP

The First Lady said he was wrong. I wouldn't say it was an out and out quarrel but it was a strong difference of opinion. That's off the record.

JANE

Why, you fit in the State Department fine!

PHILIP

Yes, they taught me how to say that. They take you in a small room and lock the door and show you just how to do it. (*Mouthing it*) That's-off-the-record. It only took me twenty minutes. It's not hard.

JANE

You do it very well.

PHILIP

It's nothing! A knack, mostly!

JANE

What else happened?

PHILIP

That's all. We went home.

JANE

Right after dinner?

PHILIP

Pretty soon. He gets up at six.

JANE

That doesn't sound very memorable.

PHILIP

Well, Presidents don't recite the Gettysburg Address every night. It was memorable to me. I'm very impressed with myself.

JANE

You do look kind of stuffy.

PHILIP

You're jealous.

JANE

I can ask my doctor whether to take saccharine. And get a better opinion.

PHILIP

Maybe you'll be invited sometime. I'll do what I can.

JANE

Don't bother. And I don't think I'm going to vote for him. I expect more interesting dinner talk from my President.

PHILIP

Now that I think of it, there was some mention of you at the table.

JANE

Of me?

PHILIP

I don't know how it came up that you were Alfred's sister-in-law, but you were the topic of conversation almost as long as the saccharine.

JANE

Well, now! Don't leave anything out.

PHILIP

The President's seen you often, and he thinks you're charming. That was the word, "charming." You don't seem very pleased.

JANE

"Charming" isn't a very strong word. Not in the theatre.

PHILIP

The President isn't in the theatre.

JANE

Yes, that's true.

PHILIP

The First Lady thought you were "extremely exciting." That was her exact phrase.

JANE

That's better. Well, I'll vote for her. (*Pause*)

PHILIP

(*Hesitant*) I've—taken a suite here in the hotel.

JANE

Really?

PHILIP

I figured as long as I took that job I'd need a permanent place in New York. You can't ask them to keep a suite free just for week-ends.

JANE

No, you can't. Is it a nice apartment?

PHILIP

Yes. It's a floor below. Would you care to see it?

JANE

My mother said never to go to men's apartments. (*Wryly*) She never mentioned anything about them coming to mine.

PHILIP

She was a wonderful woman.

JANE

If she's looking down, she's frowning.

PHILIP

(*He takes her hand*) She's smiling.

JANE

Well, if you're sure.

PHILIP

Is it necessary to make a reservation at that Italian place? I wouldn't want to be turned away.

JANE

I've made one.

PHILIP

(*Eyeing her*) You're remarkable. Truly remarkable. What would you like to do tomorrow? After rehearsal.

JANE

There's no rehearsal tomorrow.

PHILIP

No?

JANE

Or fittings. Or phone calls. Everyone thinks I'm the country. (*It rings*) Almost everyone. (*She goes to the phone*) Hello? . . . Thank you, Molly. (*She hangs up*) There's a surprise! My dear sister is on her way up here!

PHILIP

I'll skip down to my place!

JANE

Yes, you'd better! She won't say long! I'll call you! (*He starts*) Don't forget your hat!

PHILIP

Good for you! (*He gets it, goes toward the hall door, and the door buzzer sounds*)

JANE

For heaven's sake!

PHILIP

She must have been in the elevator.

JANE

(*Towards the guest bedroom*) Get in there!

PHILIP

Am I supposed to go under the bed?

JANE

Don't be funny! That's my sister! (*He goes into guest room. She closes the door. Crossing to admit Margaret at hall door*) It's bad enough my mother knows. (*She opens the door for Margaret*)

MARGARET

(*Strolling in*) Hello.

JANE

Hello. What are you doing in town?

MARGARET

I had some errands. I've only got a minute. (*She sits, leisurely taking off her gloves. Jane waits*) What are you doing with yourself?

JANE

Doing with myself? I'm rehearsing!

MARGARET

That all?

JANE

What more would you expect?

MARGARET

I merely asked what you were doing with yourself besides the rehearsals? I'm curious how you spend your day.

JANE

Well, if you're interested. I get up in the morning, and I brush my teeth. Then I have my breakfast, and I read the morning paper—

MARGARET

What about Mister Philip Clair?

JANE

What about him?

MARGARET

Doesn't he come in someplace, between the brushing the teeth and the breakfast?

JANE

What—are—you talking about?

MARGARET

The reason it's always been difficult for me to know how good an actress you are is because I know you so well.

JANE

I saw Mister Clair at your home for dinner Friday before last!

MARGARET

Oh, I know that. I was there. I know more than that. You two were so cool and polite to each other that a stranger passing by could look through the window and know you were carrying on!

JANE

Carrying on?

MARGARET

Oh, come now!

JANE

Is this a fishing expedition of yours?

MARGARET

Sister knows all! All!

JANE

(*Carefully*) Name something.

MARGARET

He was here last week-end, and the week-end before. I don't know about this week-end, yet.

JANE

How do you know?

MARGARET

Alfred.

JANE

(*Unbelieving*) You mean Philip told Alfred he was here?

MARGARET

Not Philip, the F.B.I.

JANE

The F.B.I.!

MARGARET

The F.B.I. doesn't let new members of the State Department wander around without knowing where they go.

JANE

For heaven's sake! What else do they know?

MARGARET

Whatever you did, they know. Take my word for it.

JANE

Well, the country's come to a fine state! Peeping Toms! Spying!

MARGARET

It's 'security,' dear. It's all for our own good.

JANE

I've met J. Edgar Hoover at dinner parties! I'll be so embarrassed I won't be able to look at him!

MARGARET

He has other things on his mind.

JANE

You'd think he'd have the decency not to go out to dinner parties and embarrass people.

MARGARET

If J. Edgar Hoover didn't go everywhere in Washington he knew something about the people, he'd starve to death!

JANE

Has Alfred said anything?

MARGARET

You've made Alfred very happy. You've gotten Mister Clair into the State Department.

JANE

Real patriotic of me. Like Nathan Hale.

MARGARET

If I remember my history, the contribution wasn't exactly the same, dear.

JANE

(*Looking at her watch*) You haven't much time to catch your train!

MARGARET

(*Seriously*) Jane, I didn't come here to show you I've been snooping. I've something unpleasant to say and I'm dreading it.

JANE

(*Aware of the new tone*) What is it?

MARGARET

I saw your Mister Clair having lunch with a woman at the Mayflower last Tuesday.

JANE

I don't own him, Margaret. And having lunch!

MARGARET

I was curious who the woman was, and I started some enquiries. This is the unpleasant part. Mister Clair is a married man.

JANE

(*Touched by her sister's solicitude*) I know, darling.

MARGARET

(*Looking at her searchingly*) You're acting now. How do you know?

JANE

He told me.

MARGARET

Did he, really? Well, that's novel. Is he getting a divorce?

JANE

He never can. (*Margaret is quite unhappy*)

MARGARET

Well . . .

JANE

I'm over twenty-one darling.

MARGARET

Yes, you are. You are. Are you doing the right thing?

JANE

I don't know. I haven't any choice. I did have in the beginning, but not now.

MARGARET

You love him?

JANE

Terribly.

MARGARET

And you're happy? That's not the same as being in love.

JANE

I've never been happier.

MARGARET

Well, that'll do for me. I guess it'll have to. (*She kisses her sister*) Goodbye, Janie.

JANE
Goodbye, big sister. And thank you.

MARGARET
'Bye. (*She starts out*)

JANE
How old was the woman he was having lunch with at the Mayflower last Tuesday?

MARGARET
Too young for him. Don't get hurt, dear. Be sure you leave him first. (*She's out through hall door. We hear the door close. Jane is thoughtful a moment. She wrenches herself out of it. She goes to the guest room door, Left. She knocks, and opens it, part of the way*)

JANE
Coast is clear! (*No answer. She half steps into the room, calling*) Philip! (*She comes out, followed by Philip*) Were you listening?

PHILIP
(*Pleasant, but oddly restrained*) No, I wasn't.

JANE
Not a word?

PHILIP
I was in the dressing room. I couldn't hear a sound.

JANE
Would you like one drink here? I can make you a vermouth. I'll chill it just as they do.

PHILIP
I don't think so. (*Jane looks at him searchingly*)

JANE

What is it?

PHILIP

What's what?

JANE

There's something the matter? You're all clouded up.

PHILIP

I'm sorry. I don't mean to be.

JANE

You may not mean to be, but you are. What is it you heard that offended you?

PHILIP

I didn't hear anything. I was in the dressing room. I couldn't.

JANE

You must have heard something.

PHILIP

I give you my word. I take an oath I don't know whether it was a man or a woman.

JANE

A man? (*He knows he's tipped his hand*) Don't you believe it was my sister?

PHILIP

I didn't say it wasn't.

JANE

You're implying it.

PHILIP

I have no right to ask whether it was your sister or not. It's none of my business.

JANE

No, it isn't. But do you think it was?

PHILIP

If you say so, I'm sure it was.

JANE

(*She sits*) Well, this is an unexpected development. (*There is a most uncomfortable silence*) Or is it? I wonder if I haven't been waiting for it?

PHILIP

Waiting?

JANE

Yes. We were getting along too well. (*He says nothing*) I counted on something, I was just hoping it would be tiny.

PHILIP

Why were you counting on anything?

JANE

It's the way things seem to go, between men and women. Eventually, some obstacle.

PHILIP

It's not an obstacle that can't be surmounted.

JANE

Jealousy's awfully difficult. (*A moment*) I'm rather a coward. I dread being unhappy.

PHILIP

It's a fear common to all of us.

JANE

You'll never know whether it really was my sister.

PHILIP

I said it was none of my business.

JANE

(*Unhappily*) That's not true. It was your business. It very
much was your business. (*There is quite a pause. And the
outer door is heard, and Margaret appears, key in hand*)

MARGARET

I forgot my—(*She sees him*) gloves! Why, hello!

PHILIP

(*Lost*) Hello. (*Silence*)

MARGARET

(*Helping*) You must have just come up in the other elevator.

PHILIP

Yes, that's it.

MARGARET

I guess we passed each other.

PHILIP

We must have. How are you?

MARGARET

Fine.

PHILIP

And the family?

MARGARET

(*Taking her gloves*) I'm afraid I haven't time for all that. (*A look to Jane*) Goodbye, dear.

JANE

Goodbye.

PHILIP

Goodbye.

MARGARET

(*She stops at the hall exit*) This God-given faculty I have for the wrong thing is beginning to frighten me. (*And she's out. We hear the door closing*)

PHILIP

Do I look as ridiculous as I feel?

JANE

Yes, you do.

PHILIP

(*He comes to her. A plea*) Can you forgive me?

JANE

It's not a matter of forgiving. Can we be happy?

PHILIP

I do have a jealous streak. But I'll get over it. I'll root it out. You'll never be subjected to this indignity again. (*She looks at him a long moment. They go into each other's arms. Evidently she is crying. Philip is moved*) You do love me!

JANE

No, I don't!

PHILIP

(*Telling her*) You do! Take my word for it. I'm older, I'm smarter.

JANE

(*Never moving from his arms*) I don't want to be made un-happy, but if you'd left I'd've been unhappy anyway. I'm too far in, I might as well go on.

PHILIP

I'll never make you unhappy again.

JANE

Oh, yes you will.

PHILIP

No, I won't. (*She straightens. She takes his handkerchief and dabs*) A woman won't believe it, but she's quite attractive after she's been crying.

JANE

I'm sure.

PHILIP

It stirs something in him.

JANE

Stir yourself some other way.

PHILIP

Do you know I'd made up my mind you'd never discover my jealousy? The first night I'd met you. I took a solemn oath, in my bathroom. Really! Raised my hand and everything.

JANE

(*Blowing*) You shouldn't take an oath in a bathroom.

PHILIP

Maybe that was what was wrong with it.

JANE

If you wanted to know whether it was a man or not, all you had to do was listen.

PHILIP

I didn't want to listen. I didn't want to hear his voice. And I was sure it was a man.

JANE

How could you have been sure?

PHILIP

You said it was your sister coming up, and Alfred told me specifically he and Margaret were not going to be in New York for the week-end.

JANE

I see. Well, there was some justification then.

PHILIP

It's happened before without the justification.

JANE

What did you mean to do, when this—man—left? Were you going to just carry it off?

PHILIP

I was determined you weren't going to know I was jealous. I was going to act gay, charming, inscrutable.

JANE

You were? And that was it? I have seen a great many perform-
ances in my day, and I am free to say your interpretation
stands by itself.

PHILIP

Oh, I knew I wasn't hiding it! I could feel myself flushing.
And it was getting worse! In the next few minutes I'd've
banged your present down on the table, said something very
cutting and unclever, and stalked out!

JANE

(*Brightly*) Present? What present?

PHILIP

(*He takes it out of his pocket and tosses it in her lap*) I'm
going to make myself a drink! And not vermouth! (*He goes to
the liquor tray, while Jane unwraps the tiny box*)

JANE

(*Bright, happy, excited, reading in reverse*) Oh, you shouldn't
have! No, no, I wish you hadn't! I don't take presents from
men! You shouldn't have, you shouldn't have. No, no! (*She
finally has it open. Genuine*) Oh, no!

PHILIP

I hope you like it.

JANE

Like it? It's beautiful! Now look here, I *am* crazy about sur-
prises, but this is more in the nature of a shock!

PHILIP

The man said it was a friendship ring. We're friends.

JANE

Yes, we are. He was a nice man. (*Holding it off*) This early in the game we're only supposed to be up to flowers and candy.

PHILIP

I thought we'd skipped a few steps.

JANE

Not that many.

PHILIP

It seems a little bunched up to me, but as long as you like it—

JANE

(*Waving her fingers, admiring the ring*) You cannot bunch up rubies. Your taste is exquisite.

PHILIP

I don't get credit for the taste. A woman picked it out. (*His back is to her. She is alert, frozen*)

JANE

(*Normal voice*) A woman?

PHILIP

(*Oblivious*) My niece. She works on Vogue. We were having lunch at the Mayflower last Tuesday, and I asked her to help.

JANE

(*Back on the ring*) Your niece. (*She smiles*) I don't understand people being jealous. I'm glad I'm not.

PHILIP

Don't worry about it, I'm jealous enough for two. (*He drinks*)

JANE

(*Still shining the ring, waving her fingers*) Twinkle, twinkle. (*The phone rings. Jane goes to it*) That'll be Margaret from the corner drug store. (*Into phone*) Hello? . . . (*She smiles, looking at Philip*)

PHILIP

I'd love to listen.

JANE

(*Into phone, pleasantly*) I wish you wouldn't. . . . Please don't come up . . . I wouldn't let you in . . . Not even flowers! Good-bye, dear.

PHILIP

What was that about the flowers?

JANE

That wasn't my sister. (*A pause*) It was an ex- (*A slight emphasis on the next word*)—suitor. He used to be partial to *red* roses. (*She watches him carefully*) You're clouding up again.

PHILIP

Am I?

JANE

(*Soft*) He's not here, Philip. You are. You're the one I want to be with. Doesn't that help?

PHILIP

(*Trying*) You didn't have to call him 'dear.'

JANE

I was very fond of him. Once. And we're still friends.

PHILIP

(*Trying*) What did he call you about?

JANE

He wanted to send back a ring I had returned to him. A friendship ring. You're clouding up again. Steady, darling. Maybe counting'll help. I'll start with you. Come, one, two—

PHILIP

(*Through his teeth*) I'm up to thirty now!

JANE

Well then, thirty-one, thirty-two—

TOGETHER

Thirty-three, thirty-four, thirty-five—

CURTAIN

ACT TWO

Scene Two

Six months later. Bowls of yellow roses are in different locations. Annie and Carl are seated, checking items from lists they hold.

ANNIE

Twelve cases of champagne.

CARL

Twelve cases of champagne. Where are they?

ANNIE

In the guest bathroom. They're up to the ceiling. You can't even get in.

CARL

Everything he buys, he buys a dozen. Doesn't he think they'll sell him any less? What's next?

ANNIE

Abercrombie and Fitch.

CARL

(*Looking for the name on the next page*) Abercrombie and Fitch.

ANNIE

Rowboat.

CARL

Just one? Not a dozen? (*Checking*) Rowboat.

ANNIE

Two fishing rods.

CARL

(*Checking*) Two fishing rods.

ANNIE

Two extra reels.

CARL

Two extra reels.

ANNIE

Two creels.

CARL

Two creels.

ANNIE

What's a creel?

CARL

A little basket that holds the fish.

ANNIE

Wading boots? Size six and eleven.

CARL

They don't need boots for fishing in a lake. They made a mistake.

ANNIE

They made no mistakes. They've talked everything over a hundred times. They sit here until three in the morning, like two kids going camping. Put down wading boots. (*He checks it off*) Mosquito netting?

CARL

How much?

ANNIE

Twenty yards.

CARL

(*Writing*) Twenty yards.

ANNIE

(*Reading*) Canned—worms?

CARL

(*Checking*) Canned worms.

ANNIE

Is that right?

CARL

I got two cases.

ANNIE

Haven't they got worms in Maine?

CARL

These are imported worms.

ANNIE

Hmm.

CARL

Don't you think we should wait a while with all this ordering until she knows for sure she can rent the house?

ANNIE

Don't even say that for a joke! (*She knocks on wood*) She's going to get the house. She'd die if she didn't get it.

CARL

You have to face facts. The owner doesn't want to rent it. The real estate agent was up here and told her. I heard him say it.

ANNIE

She went to see the owner. She'll come back with the house.

CARL

I'm a realist. If a man doesn't want to rent, he doesn't want to rent. Why can't it be another house? That's not the only house in Maine for rent.

ANNIE

She's got her heart set on this one. He'll rent! Take my word for it! (*She knocks wood*)

CARL

What good does that do?

ANNIE

What harm does it do?

CARL

That's a good point. You've just put your finger on the big practical reason for being religious. If there's something in it, fine, if not, what do you lose? All you've lost is—

ANNIE

Enough! (*Pointing to the list*) Canned worms!

CARL

(*Seriously*) Anna. What's going to come of this?

ANNIE

Of what?

CARL

Of Miss Kimball and Mister Clair?

ANNIE

What has to come of it?

CARL

It can't go on like this.

ANNIE

Why not?

CARL

A man, a wife, another woman.

ANNIE

(*Solemn, too*) I think about it, too.

CARL

Some day he'll have to leave her.

ANNIE

At least she's had the last six months. That they can't take away. She's never looked so good, she's never acted so good, she's ten years younger. She's happy. And she deserves to be happy. Maybe there'll be no day of reckoning for her.

CARL

Life has a rule. What you put in, you take out.

ANNIE

Who is she hurting? And she's not taking, she's giving. She was lonely so long maybe this happiness is what's been coming to her. Maybe now the books are coming out even.

CARL

Maybe. (*He knocks wood*) What can it hurt? (*The outer door is heard opening and closing. Philip appears, placing the key, on his key ring, back in his pocket. Annie and Carl get up*)

PHILIP

(*Familiarly*) Good evening, Annie, Carl.

CARL

Good evening, Mister Clair.

ANNIE

Good evening, Mister Clair. You're early.

PHILIP

I took the two o'clock. Anybody home?

ANNIE

She ought to be here any minute. (*Carl goes out pantry door*) She went to see the man who owns the house in Maine.

PHILIP

Ah, yes.

ANNIE

Do you think she'll get it?

PHILIP

I'll bet on her. She'll charm it out of him.

ANNIE

And then she had a fitting appointment at Main Bocher. Shall I fix you a drink?

PHILIP

I'll do it myself, Annie. (*He goes to fix the drink*) Everything else all right?

ANNIE

Everything's fine, Mister Clair.

PHILIP

Leading man get over his cold?

ANNIE

Oh yes.

PHILIP

It's remarkable Miss Kimball didn't catch it.

ANNIE

I don't think actors catch anything from each other. They become immune to germs. (*Shakes her head*) If they didn't—ah! (*She goes out pantry door. Philip takes his drink, walks to the chair, would put the drink down, reminds himself, crosses to the table, pulls out the drawer, takes out a coaster, goes back to the chair, puts the coaster on the small table, and the drink on it, and sits. He picks up the phone*)

PHILIP

(*Into phone*) Hello Molly. Any calls for me? Get me Main Bocher, please. (*He takes his cigarette case out, opens it, sees he has no cigarettes. He gets up, crosses to another table, opens the second drawer, and takes out a pack of cigarettes. He goes back to the phone, listening and opening the pack of cigarettes*) Would you connect me with Miss Kimball, please? She's in one of the fitting rooms. (*Remembers*) Miss Davis' room! (*He lights the cigarette*) Hello. . . . Hello, Miss Davis. This is Mister Clair . . . Oh. How long ago did she leave? . . .

Look here, I don't like being avoided this way. If you and Miss Kimball don't care for my suggestions I think you should come right out with it instead of sneaking around behind my back . . . (*The outer door is heard closing, and Jane appears, with a dress box*)

JANE

(*Putting the box down*) Who are you talking to?

PHILIP

(*To her*) Miss Davis. (*Into phone*) No, I just said 'Miss Davis' to Miss Kimball. She just came in. 'Bye. (*He gets up*)

JANE

How long have you been here?

PHILIP

Two minutes. (*They kiss. It's a kiss of a six months relationship. Annie enters, will take the dress box and exit Right*)

JANE

(*Looking a him carefully*) You're early. Everything all right?

PHILIP

Certainly.

JANE

Let's see. (*She grimaces, as one does to show teeth. Philip shows his teeth, waiting for her opinion. She's doubtful*) It's a little darker than the others.

PHILIP

It is not. (*He goes to a mirror. She does, too*)

JANE

I say it is.

PHILIP

(*Looking at his tooth in the mirror*) It's your imagination.

JANE

You should have gone to my dentist.

PHILIP

This fellow's a fine dentist.

JANE

What's he doing in Washington?

PHILIP

Oh, you snob. (*Still in the mirror*) He's only been the dentist to three presidents.

JANE

I'm a snob?

PHILIP

I can't tell it from the others. It's only because you know it's capped. (*Turning back*) Do you know I can't chew gum now? It's plastic and gum sticks to it.

JANE

What do you care? You don't chew gum.

PHILIP

In case I feel like it. How did you do with the fellow who owns the house in Maine?

JANE

Oh, I'm so mad I can't talk about it. I went to see him, all prepared to sit up pretty and beg, and he was so rude I just turned on my heel and left.

PHILIP

What do you mean 'rude'? You mean 'fresh'?

JANE

Oh, it doesn't matter. He didn't have the only house in
Maine. I went to another agent, and I found a beautiful cot-
tage, with a boat landing, and a speed boat and everything!
And at a cheaper rental!

PHILIP

Well, you are fickle. You were going to die if you didn't get
just that house. Nothing else would do.

JANE

Well, I'll live. (*She smiles*) Excuse me, dear, I'll be a few minutes. (*She exits into her bedroom. Philip thinks, displeased,
takes a tiny address book from his pocket, and goes to the
phone*)

PHILIP

Molly, may I have Madison—6-2121. . . . Hello, I'd like to speak
to Mister Waverly. . . . (*Jane appears in her door. Her arms
are folded, she's smiling wisely. Philip's back is to her*) Waverly? This is Clair! . . . Listen, you! I bought that house from
you with the understanding you were to rent it to Miss Kimball! Wasn't that simple enough for you to carry out? And
what the hell do you mean by being fresh to her!

JANE

Ah hah!

PHILIP

I've got a good mind to—(*The 'Ah hah' has just sunk in. He
turns and sees Jane smiling at him. She waves her fingers*) Oh,

excuse me, Mister Waverly, I have been made the victim of a
practical joke. I apologize. . . . I said I apologize! I—(*He has
been hung up on*) Funny today, aren't we?

PHILIP

JANE

I had a notion you bought it. He rented it to me too easily.
And too cheap.

PHILIP

Cheaply, dear.

JANE

Why did you have to buy it? Do you have to buy everything
you see?

PHILIP

It looked like a good investment.

JANE

Why, you've never even seen it!

PHILIP

Well, you described it to me.

JANE

You didn't have to buy it! I told you I'd be able to rent it!
They just were fiddling for a little more money!

PHILIP

That's all right, I don't own anything in Maine.

JANE

What's that got to do with it? You don't own anything in
Honolulu!

PHILIP

Yes, I do. Another fellow and I own a canning factory. A small one. See, you don't understand these things, dear. It's called 'scattering your risk.' You invest in different places.

JANE

(*She sits on the sofa*) You're not going to turn this into being a smart business move!

PHILIP

(*Also sitting on the sofa*) Yes, I am. Yes, it is.

JANE

How much did you pay for it?

PHILIP

Never mind. I made a very shrewd deal.

JANE

Let's hear it.

PHILIP

He wanted thirty-five thousand, I offered him thirty. We tossed. (*He grins*) I won.

JANE

Thirty! He once tried to sell it to me for twenty-five.

PHILIP

When was that?

JANE

Last week!

PHILIP

Oh, last week. Inflation you know. Money getting cheaper and all that.

JANE

Are you sure you made money in the banking business?

PHILIP

Some.

JANE

It must be rather simple.

PHILIP

Don't tell anyone. (*She snuggles in his arms*)

JANE

I know why you spend so much money on me.

PHILIP

(*In the embrace*) Why?

JANE

It's your conscience. You feel you have to make it up to me.

PHILIP

That's not true.

JANE

I read that in a magazine article. About men who keep
women.

PHILIP

Shame on you. I'm not keeping you. I give you presents because I like to please you.

JANE

(*Still in his embrace. She looks at him a long moment*) I love
you. (*They kiss. Still with their arms around each other*) I
wish you had no money. I wish we were on a desert island.

PHILIP

(*Tenderly*) We are on a desert island.

JANE

You always say the right thing. (*She puts her face on his chest*)
There was a joke in the magazine about a desert island. (*Flat,
reciting, their arms about each other*) If a woman was to be
stranded on a desert island, and she had her choice of one
man, who should she choose?

PHILIP

Clark Gable?

JANE

No.

PHILIP

Einstein?

JANE

No.

PHILIP

I give up.

JANE

An obstetrician.

PHILIP

What kind of magazine was that?

JANE

I don't know. I read it under the dryer. (*Philip gets up*) All
right, out with it.

PHILIP

Out with what?

JANE

The reason you're early. You're the most transparent man I
ever met. I hope the State Department's not trusting you with
any secrets.

PHILIP

You'd be surprised.

JANE

Let's hear one.

PHILIP

You'd be surprised, Mata Hari.

JANE

Just tell me whether it's unpleasant or not. I can never wait.
I always look at the end of the book.

PHILIP

You have no restraint. (*She smiles at him, intimate*)

JANE

Begin!

PHILIP

Well, the Secretary called me in this morning. And gave me
a cigar. He said he was very pleased with me—(*Modestly*) up
to now, anyway—

JANE

Well, I should think so!

PHILIP

And he wanted to know if I'd accept a change of assignment.
(*A moment, different tone*) In London.

JANE

London!

PHILIP

That's exactly what I said.

JANE

(*Quietly*) You refused him of course.

PHILIP

I did.

JANE

(*Relieved*) Give him his cigar back.

PHILIP

I said we'd had an understanding of what my duties would be, and where, and it would be inconvenient for me to change.

JANE

Very inconvenient. They can't make you go? It isn't like the army?

PHILIP

No, they can't make me go.

JANE

Well, then everything is all right. (*She kisses his cheek*) Darling, don't frighten Jane any more. (*To change the subject*) I have bought a dress with a money back guarantee that strong men will wail piteously as I go by—(*She has been watching his expression all during the forced joking. There seems to be some doubt*) You were definite about refusing. Weren't you?

PHILIP

No. I left it open.

JANE

Why?

PHILIP

I wanted your advice.

JANE

Well, you have it. And tear up your passport, too.

PHILIP

I omitted a sidelight.

JANE

I don't think it would influence me.

PHILIP

You do want to hear the case for both sides?

JANE

(*Fearful*) Not especially.

PHILIP

The man I'd go instead of is the author of a very complicated monetary pact—

JANE

You're losing me, darling.

PHILIP

It's been his work for many years. And now it's ready to be closed.

JANE

Let him close it.

PHILIP

It takes some negotiating.

JANE

Let him.

PHILIP

He means to. He thinks he's going to London. The trouble is if he goes he'll never get back. There's some question whether he'd live long enough to finish negotiating.

JANE

(*All compassion*) Oh!

PHILIP

It's more touching than that. He knows he's dying. And he thinks we don't know. And he means to keep it from us.

JANE

Oh no!

PHILIP

He's a wonderful man. What do I tell the Secretary, Jane? (*Saying it for her*) What about someone else? I'm a good cut under this man, the next under me is two cuts. Take my immodest word for it.

JANE

(*A pause*) How long would it be?

PHILIP

At least three months. Maybe four or five.

JANE

Five months! (*She looks at him. Quietly, knowing*) You've already said you'll go.

PHILIP

It'll go by quicker than you think.

JANE

That's not true. Why do people always say it? It'll be longer than I think. Much longer.

PHILIP

I feel as badly as you do, dear.

JANE

Want to bet? (*She gets up*) When do you leave?

PHILIP

There's a whole commission going. We sail tomorrow on the Elizabeth.

JANE

Tomorrow! Why, it is as bad as the army!

PHILIP

I won't be with you for your birthday.

JANE

Or for Maine. Why did you buy the house?

PHILIP

It was before I knew. Maybe I'll be able to join you there the last month.

JANE

I won't go without you.

PHILIP

I'd like you to. There's an even chance I'll get there before the summer's over. Better than an even chance. (*Jane is very unhappy. She walks. She thinks. Finally*)

JANE

(*Quietly*) I can come to London in a few weeks.

PHILIP

Jane! How?

JANE

They're buying the play for pictures. They'll gladly put the movie star in it.

PHILIP

Jane, it's not my place to urge you—

JANE

I don't need any urging.

PHILIP

(*He goes to her*) I don't know if deep down I haven't been hoping—. We'll be very discreet.

JANE

I don't care. (*She sits. They kiss. She stays in his arms*)

PHILIP

Dear Jane. (*A moment. She straightens*)

JANE

Philip—

PHILIP

Yes, dear?

JANE

Could you possibly get a divorce and marry me? (*She looks at him a long moment*) Oh, God! I don't know why I said that! Please forgive me! Please! I don't know what came over me! (*She's frantic. Philip comforts her*)

PHILIP

(*Suffering*) Jane! Please don't!

JANE

I'm so ashamed! I had no right! I despise women like that! If I were a man and a woman put me in this position I'd never forgive her!

PHILIP

Jane, it's nothing— (*She slips to her knees*)

JANE

Promise you'll put this out of your mind! You'll forget this ever happened! Promise me! It never happened!

PHILIP

It never happened.

JANE

I never said it!

PHILIP

You never said it!

JANE

And we'll never refer to it as long as we live!

PHILIP

We'll never refer to it!

JANE

I've done it again! 'As long as we live!' That's the same thing!
You're a free agent, Philip! You can go when you please! I
have no strings on you!

PHILIP

I do love you, Jane.

JANE

(*Her face in his lap*) I don't see how. I'm not worthy of you.
I'm not entitled to you. Why don't you get up and leave? I
wouldn't blame you.

PHILIP

Maybe later. My darling. (*He swivels her face up. He gives
her his handkerchief*) You're beautiful when you cry!

JANE

I'm sure. Pink eyes are so becoming. Oh, I'm going to give a
hell of a performance tonight. (*The chimes of St. Timothy's
are heard*) It's six o'clock. I ought to start. (*She doesn't move*)

PHILIP

(*Listening to the chimes*) I'm sorry to miss your birthday. Tomorrow night, at the stroke of midnight, we'll drink a toast
to each other. Will you remember?

JANE

I'm going to drink the whole twelve cases.

PHILIP

(*He looks at his watch*) On the first sound of the chimes, raise your glass. Where will you be? I want to picture you.

JANE

The fireplace is usual. I did it in a play ten years ago. I was wonderful in it. (*The door buzzer is heard*)

PHILIP

There they are.

JANE

They know, of course? (*Annie enters from pantry, crosses, Rear, to open the hall door*)

PHILIP

Yes. Alfred feels very badly about it. (*Margaret and Alfred appear. Margaret in evening dress. Alfred has his handbag. Annie goes out to pantry*)

JANE

(*For Alfred's benefit*) Alfred should feel badly about it. He hoodwinked you into the State Department.

MARGARET

Hello, dear.

JANE

Hello.

ALFRED

Hello, Jane.

JANE

Hello, Judas.

ALFRED

There was no other choice.

JANE

I could've given you a list of names. Yours on top.

MARGARET

The first thing I said to him, Jane, was 'Why can't you go?'

ALFRED

Her exact words were 'Why the hell can't you go?' In front of the servants.

MARGARET

He explained he wasn't bright enough. Philip is supposed to be very clever about money.

JANE

I haven't seen any evidence of it. I think he'll bankrupt the country.

MARGARET

(*Doing her best*) We'll have a nice time tonight. We didn't want you two to be alone.

JANE

Why not, may I ask?

MARGARET

(*Flustered*) You're not taking the right attitude, Jane! The time'll go by quicker than you think—

JANE

(*Turning*) I'm going to get dressed! (*Margaret looks at the men, glares at Alfred, and marches after Jane, into master bedroom. She closes the door*)

ALFRED

I wish I was going with you. (*Alfred sits, Philip takes out a small notebook, which he consults*)

PHILIP

The group that's going tomorrow, they're using the four days on the boat for discussion. I'm not in on that. Is it all right if I fly?

ALFRED

Why, certainly.

PHILIP

I'd like the three days here.

ALFRED

Oh, of course.

PHILIP

(*Slightly self-conscious*) Tomorrow at midnight Jane and I are drinking a toast to each other. She thinks I'll be on the high seas.

ALFRED

And you'll walk in the door?

PHILIP

It ought to be quite a surprise.

ALFRED

Yes, it should be. That's very romantic. (*Philip looks to him*) I didn't mean it disparagingly. I envy you. Your—touch. (*Pause*) However, it's my belief success with women is something you're born with, and you're not entitled to any of the credit. You either have it or haven't it. It's a gift. Like playing the piano.

PHILIP

Not being able to play the piano, I can't say.

ALFRED

You may have worked out your own little refinements, but basically it's what you're born with.

PHILIP

Refinements?

ALFRED

Well, I mean the many little things you do to please a woman. And I'm not referring to presents. I know men who spend more than you, and are better looking, and bat zero. I'm one of them.

PHILIP

Really?

ALFRED

I don't mean I'm better looking. I mean I'm one of the other group. And I mean before I was married.

PHILIP

I see.

ALFRED

I'm not embarrassing you?

PHILIP

Not at all.

ALFRED

It's an interesting subject.

PHILIP

It's very popular.

ALFRED

There's one thing I'm curious about. I'm hesitant about mentioning it for fear you'll be offended.

PHILIP

(*He's willing to quit this*) That might be true.

ALFRED

I'm going to have to chance it.

PHILIP

Well, if I can't stop you—

ALFRED

I don't mean it as censure. As I said, I'm only curious. (*A moment*) Why do you pretend to be a married man when you're not? (*There is quite a pause*)

PHILIP

How did you know?

ALFRED

They make quite a security check.

PHILIP

Do you mean to tell Jane?

ALFRED

Of course not. What do you take me for?

PHILIP

Her brother-in-law, for one thing.

ALFRED

I'm not her guardian. And she's over twenty-one. A good deal over.

PHILIP

(*Thinking, far off*) You cad.

ALFRED

Well, speaking of cads—

PHILIP

(*Deciding to explain*) By my lights, I'm quite honorable.

ALFRED

(*Delicately*) I'm sure you are, I'm just not clear on your reasoning.

PHILIP

I meet a woman I'm attracted to. I'm single. I court her. We're old enough, I accept favors. Eventually, she'd like to get married. I then say I'm not the marrying kind. I don't believe that's honorable. It's usual, but not honorable.

ALFRED

I follow you. So far.

PHILIP

I don't care to be married. 'Don't care' is an understatement. I will not be married! On the other hand, I don't care to renounce women.

ALFRED

I follow that, too.

PHILIP

This puts me in an odd moral position.

ALFRED

Yes, it does.

PHILIP

I mean spiritually morally.

ALFRED

There's a difference.

PHILIP

Since I have no intention of getting married I feel honor bound to declare myself. In the beginning.

ALFRED

Before the favors?

PHILIP

Before! That's where the honor comes in! How shall I declare myself? By a speech? Every woman thinks she'll be the exception. If anything, it excites her. I'm more honorable than that. I really take myself off the marriage market! I say I am married! I'm married and I can't get a divorce! Can anything be fairer and more above board? I say I'm an honorable man! I know I'm an honorable man! God, if you knew the wonderful women I've lost with my damned honor! (*Quite a pause*)

ALFRED

You know, I think the State Department's got you in the wrong job.

PHILIP

I don't want to get married! It's my life and it's a free country and this is the way I want to live it!

ALFRED

I know there's a big hole in your argument. I haven't come to it yet but there must be.

PHILIP

Not morally.

ALFRED

You keep saying 'morally.' You've got it wrong. You're the exception, you know! Many people do get married!

PHILIP

I don't resent it.

ALFRED

That's very tolerant of you.

PHILIP

I just ask them to return the indifference.

ALFRED

Don't you think anybody ought to be married?

PHILIP

I like to see people married! Other people!

ALFRED

You're just against marriage for yourself?

PHILIP

Indeed I am! And whether you believe it or not, I love Jane! I love her more than I've ever loved any woman! But I wouldn't marry her if you held a gun to my head!

ALFRED

I haven't any gun. Anyway, I don't think it's the brother-in-law's place. Has to be a blood relative. (*Philip sits*)

PHILIP

(*Quieter*) I'm sorry you found out.

ALFRED

I am too. I didn't mean to, you know. It was in the F.B.I. report. It doesn't affect my regard for you.

PHILIP

It probably does, even if you don't think so. We only have one set of morals.

ALFRED

My morals are adjustable. I've been in the State Department a long time. (*The Down Right door opens and Margaret enters*)

MARGARET

I thought you were dressing.

PHILIP

I was just leaving. (*He gets up*)

ALFRED

We've been discussing things. Life. Very interesting.

MARGARET

What is?

ALFRED

Life. You'd be surprised.

PHILIP

(*Starting*) I'll only be a few minutes. (*Jane comes through the master bedroom door, having heard Philip's voice. She wears a dressing robe. All are conscious of this admission of intimacy*)

JANE

Philip, you'll find your dress shirts in the large cabinet. (*Philip just nods*) I also bought you some more shorts, you were running low. Don't look so embarrassed. Goodbye, dear.

PHILIP

Goodbye. (*He goes out the hall entrance. The door is heard*)

ALFRED

If anyone asks you real quickly, you're not an introvert.

JANE

That's all right isn't it?

ALFRED

Well, you'll never get ulcers.

MARGARET

But everyone else will! (*To Jane*) Well, go on, Jane. Tell him.

JANE

When Philip steps off the Elizabeth in Southampton, I'm going to be on the dock to meet him.

ALFRED

What's that?

JANE

You heard me.

MARGARET

You heard her.

ALFRED

I was hoping I didn't.

MARGARET

You were wrong.

JANE

You'll have to get me on an airplane, Alfred. Use influence.

ALFRED

Jane, be practical.

JANE

I am practical. I will not be separated from him for three months.

MARGARET

You're talking like a school girl!

JANE

A school girl can afford to wait three months!

MARGARET

See that expression on her face? The first time we saw it was when she was five years old, and we couldn't budge her then.

ALFRED

Did Philip ask you to come to London?

JANE

Philip? He'd never! His first concern was how discreet we'd be, so my reputation wouldn't be injured. He's the most considerate, unselfish, honorable person that ever lived!

MARGARET

(*Flat*) I'm voting for him for President! (*To Alfred*) Well, say something! You're a diplomat! Talk her out of it!

ALFRED

What do you advise? Just start me off.

JANE

Please don't say anything, Alfred. Please. Just get me the plane reservation.

ALFRED

Well, I'll have to say this much. There's no use your flying to England to meet the Elizabeth when it docks, because he won't be on it.

JANE

He won't?

ALFRED

He has his own surprise. As you're drinking toasts to each other at midnight tomorrow, he's coming through that door.

JANE

(*Touched*) Oh!

ALFRED

So you'll have another three days together.

MARGARET

There! Three whole days! That's enough, isn't it?

JANE

No! It's not enough! He's—isn't he—! He's so— (*She can't go on. She starts to cry into her hands*)

MARGARET

Jane! (*She goes to Jane*) Oh! (*It's beginning to affect her*)

ALFRED

I'd like not to have told—and in some way I'll get blamed for this, I'm sure—but there's no use your flying there to meet him at the dock if he's not going to be on the boat in the first place. That's going to be my story, anyway. (*Jane still cries into her hands. Margaret tries to comfort her*)

MARGARET

(*A step from tears*) Jane! Get hold of yourself!

ALFRED

I don't care to be told secrets. Whenever anyone asks me, 'Would you like to hear something confidential?', I always say 'No!', and I've never regretted it.

JANE

Oh, Margaret!

MARGARET

Oh, Jane! (*Now Margaret starts to cry. Alfred looks from one to the other. He puts his hands in his pockets, uncomfortable*)

ALFRED

This is going to be quite an evening!

JANE

(*Through the crying*) He's so wonderful—

MARGARET

(*Through the crying, louder*) No, he isn't!

JANE

(*Crying*) Don't say that!

MARGARET

(*Still crying*) He's no good! He's been fooling you! He isn't married! (*There is quite a silence*)

JANE

(*Slowly*) What did you say?

MARGARET

You heard me! He's single! He's a single—(*As an epithet*) bachelor!

ALFRED

Yes, it's going to be quite an evening.

JANE

(*But fearful*) How dare you!

MARGARET

It's true! I know it's true!

JANE

(*Deadly*) How do you know?

MARGARET

I read it in the F.B.I. report on Alfred's desk! (*Jane stands there, frozen*)

ALFRED

(*He pounds on the piano*) What do you mean by reading things on my desk! You have no right to take advantage of your position as my wife to endanger the security of our government! I forbid you to come into my office unless you're announced and I'm there!

MARGARET

Oh, shut up! (*Jane has been as marble. They watch her. She turns her head toward the spot before the sofa*)

JANE

(*Quietly*) I was down on my knees, right there, begging his forgiveness because I asked him to marry me! On my knees! (*Her mouth is set in restraint as she fights for control of herself*)

ALFRED

(*In the pause*) Well, I guess we better call off the party for tonight. I'll make our excuses. I'll say that—

JANE

(*Still with the quiet intensity*) We'll not call off the party. You're not to tell him anything. We'll spend the evening just as we planned. You'll take him with you to the ballet, I'll go to the theatre and give my performance. Then we'll all have supper together. As though nothing has happened.

MARGARET

Jane, dear, wouldn't it be better—

JANE

As though nothing has happened! That's what we're going to do! (*She turns, straight, head up, and walks slowly toward her bedroom. They wait. There is a crash of glass*)

MARGARET

(*Identifying it. Simply*) Perfume bottle through her dressing mirror. (*She shakes her head*) I'd rather be anybody in the world right now than Mister Philip Clair.

ALFRED

I believe it, too.

CURTAIN

ACT THREE

ACT THREE

Scene One

Same evening. Five hours later. On rise of Curtain the stage is deserted. The light is from the hall. The hall door is heard opening, and closing. The lights are flicked on, as Jane appears, followed by Margaret and Alfred.

ALFRED

(*Limp in the chair*) I will now draw the first clear breath I've drawn all evening. (*He does*) Aaah!

MARGARET

You gave quite a performance, dear. I mean the one after the show. Too bad the critics couldn't see it.

JANE

Thank you.

ALFRED

You'll have to excuse me. I'm too old for this sort of evening. And I always was.

MARGARET

How's your stomach?

ALFRED

Still jumping. That drink I invented—bourbon and bisodol. It'll never catch on.

119

MARGARET

What impressed me was that you could swallow anything at supper. *That* was acting! I didn't eat a thing!

ALFRED

I didn't, either. But *he* ate for everybody! He certainly was in good spirits! Dancing every dance! Singing! You'd think this was his wedding night! Excuse me. (*Jane looks at him, but doesn't say anything*)

MARGARET

Jane, I'd like to say I admire the way you carried the whole thing off. You were sweet, charming, smiling—just right. When he's in England you'll write him a little note explaining you can't possibly leave your play, and the whole relationship'll peter out naturally! No scene, no fuss.

ALFRED

Yes, just right. That's the way it'll go. The immediate step, however, is how to get rid of the annoyance of tonight.

MARGARET

Tonight?

ALFRED

Certainly tonight! You don't think when he said 'Goodbye' in the elevator, that was the end of this evening? He expects to come up here!

MARGARET

He does?

ALFRED

Didn't you see all that signalling in the elevator? He expects to come up here after we're gone!

MARGARET

Well, he's not going to!

ALFRED

I'll tell you this! You're not going to outwait him!

MARGARET

We certainly shall!

ALFRED

Margaret, middle age is obscuring your memory of romance.
Not if we're here until five in the morning!

MARGARET

(*To Jane*) Is that true?

JANE

You underestimate me. Seven!

MARGARET

Well, we'll just spend the night here! That's all there is to
that!

ALFRED

Yes, I guess that's best. That'll do it to him. Call downstairs
and tell him we're in the guest room. Say you couldn't get
rid of us. (*Jane has been looking from one to the other, merely
an observer*)

MARGARET

(*To Alfred*) What kind of signalling was he doing in the elevator? I didn't see him do anything and I thought I didn't
take my eyes off him.

ALFRED

(*Showing*) He was wig wagging over our heads— (*Indicating
himself and above*) When we left—he was going to come up.
He's not very subtle.

JANE

Oh, he manages to fool people. People who think they're rather bright, too.

MARGARET

You don't have to blame yourself for anything, dear. You're a woman, and you were deceived. It happens every day. Oftener.

JANE

Not to me.

ALFRED

You know, even our staying here tonight doesn't settle the whole problem. He means to surprise you tomorrow at midnight, while you're supposedly drinking toasts to each other.

MARGARET

I'd forgotten about that. He'll be here for three days.

ALFRED

Well, I can't stay here for three days! I have to be back in Washington!

MARGARET

I can stay! I'll have some things sent down tomorrow. (*To Jane*) We'll have a nice time together. We'll make it a little visit.

JANE

I don't remember inviting you.

MARGARET

What's that?

JANE

You will please leave, and now.

MARGARET

Leave?

ALFRED

Leave? (*He looks at Margaret*)

JANE

Leave!

MARGARET

Do you mean to let him come up here?

JANE

I mean to let him come up here.

MARGARET

Why? I mean, what for? I mean, how could you? What have you got in mind?

JANE

None of your business.

MARGARET

I want to talk to you, Jane. I've known you from the day you were born, and there's one thing in your character I don't admire. You go to extremes. What do you mean to do?

ALFRED

You're a prominent person. You have to think of scandal. (*A pause*) You haven't a gun, have you?

JANE

Shooting's too good for him.

MARGARET

That's how I like to hear you talk, dear. No violence.

ALFRED

What have you in mind? (*No answer, Jane is lost in revery*)
Just give us an idea, Jane. We're family. (*Jane slowly opens
the purse in her lap, not looking at it, still thinking. Margaret
and Alfred crane to see it*) What is it? (*Jane holds up a rose*)

MARGARET

A rose?

JANE

Yes, a rose. A red rose.

ALFRED

Yes, someone sent that to our table. I saw the waiter give it to
you. I thought it was from a fan.

MARGARET

Who sent it?

JANE

(*Still off, thinking*) David sent it.

MARGARET

David? Your David? Your old David!

JANE

(*Still in her mood*) My old David.

MARGARET

I didn't see him. Why didn't you nudge me?

ALFRED

I liked David. I even fancied him for a moment as a brother-
in-law. I always meant to ask you, what ever happened to
him?

MARGARET

I'll tell you later. (*The phone rings. They all look to it*)

ALFRED

Philip! He wants to know if we're out and the coast is clear.

MARGARET

Well, we aren't and it isn't! And it's not going to be!

JANE

(*Looking at her watch*) That's not Philip. (*She gets up and goes to the phone*) It's David. I asked him to call. (*Margaret and Alfred exchange glances. Into phone, a new voice altogether*) Hello . . . Hello, David . . . Why, certainly I'm alone! . . .

ALFRED

There's no sincerity like a woman telling a lie!

JANE

(*Into phone*) It was nice seeing *you* again. . . . Tomorrow night'll be fine. . . . Anywhere you say . . . (*As though she just thought of it*) As a matter of fact I'm not too keen on going out, David. This has been a big evening, and when I'm working I don't like two in a row. Why don't you join me for supper here, after the play?

MARGARET

For heaven's sake!

JANE

(*Into phone*) . . . Let's make it eleven-thirty. . . . That's eleven-thirty. You've got it right now, eleven-thirty! Here! . . . Why, David! . . . Bye bye. (*She hangs up*)

MARGARET

Won't it be a little crowded?

ALFRED

You haven't forgotten there's another suitor coming at twelve?

JANE

No, I haven't forgotten! That's all I've been thinking of! All
night long! (*With a frightening intensity*) His walking through
that door at midnight, and surprising me with another man!
(*She clasps her hands, raises her eyes, as in prayer*) That's all
I've been thinking of! That's how I was able to swallow my
supper! That's how I was able to talk to him, to smile at him,
to dance with him, to keep from mashing him over the head
with a lamp!

MARGARET

Jane! What's gotten into you?

JANE

Tomorrow night! I can see the expression on his face! Just as
clear! The shock, the unbelief, the horror! Cuckolded! Him!
So charming, so handsome, so generous, and still she took
another! How could she? It'll be a nightmare he'll remember
the rest of his life! He'll go over it and over it, a thousand
times! And each time it'll burn deeper and deeper, until he
won't have to recall it at all! It'll just be there! How am I
going to exist until tomorrow night!

MARGARET

When I think how carefully you were brought up!

ALFRED

I'm against it! That's my considered opinion, Jane! You're playing with fire!

MARGARET

Alfred's right! You're overdoing it!

ALFRED

Let's all stay calm! Let's sleep on it! And tomorrow, when we're cooler, we'll discuss it, rationally, as becomes grown men and women.

MARGARET

Very well put, dear. We're all overwrought now, we're not thinking clearly.

JANE

(*Just as strong*) I'm thinking clearly!

MARGARET

No, you're not. You have the feeling you're a wronged woman, you're upset—

JANE

(*Through her teeth*) I am a wronged woman!

MARGARET

Well, you know what I mean—

JANE

And you know what I mean! I'm the wrongedest woman you ever saw! And I'm going to pay him back! With interest! Two or three thousand percent of interest! (*The phone rings, interrupting. Jane looks to it*) Why, there he is now! Sooner than usual! (*In irony*) So impatient! So flattering! (*She goes to the phone*)

MARGARET

Jane, we're sleeping over!

JANE

(*Into phone*) Yes, dear, they've gone. . . . Thank you for calling to say 'Good night.' (*She hangs up*) And so considerate about my reputation! He won't let the operator know he's coming up here! (*They haven't moved*) Well! Get going! He'll be here in a minute!

ALFRED

Jane! (*He sees it's hopeless*) My bag! (*He hurries to the guest room*)

MARGARET

I'm not going! And you can't make me!

JANE

Good night, sister dear!

MARGARET

You're being impulsive, Jane! I've only your interest at heart—

JANE

(*Throwing her coat*) Good night, dear.

MARGARET

I tell you this! I'm going to telephone every fifteen minutes! (*Alfred comes out of the guest room, with bag. He takes his coat*) And somebody better answer the phone or I'll be right back!

ALFRED

(*Doubtfully*) Good night, Jane. Be careful, about everything. Nothing in anger. (*To Margaret*) Hurry up, dear! If he catches us we'll be embarrassed!

MARGARET

Why should *we* be embarrassed? He's the one sneaking up here! (*At the hall door. Heavily*) Remember Mamma. (*They're out. We hear the hall door close. Jane exits into her bedroom. The stage is deserted. The outer door opens and closes, and Philip appears, putting the key chain back in his pocket. He is quite happy. He goes to the liquor tray and pours himself a drink, humming. Jane enters from her bedroom, now without her cape*)

PHILIP

Hello, darling.

JANE

Hello.

PHILIP

(*Still at the drinks*) One for you?

JANE

No, thanks.

PHILIP

(*Coming to her*) Good evening, darling.

JANE

It's not the beginning of the evening.

PHILIP

It is for me. (*He kisses her on the cheek*)

JANE

That's very thoughtful of you, not letting the telephone operator know you're coming up here.

PHILIP

It's the least I can do.

JANE

(*Emphasis on 'small'*) It's typical of you. Consideration in small things.

PHILIP

(*Oblivious*) Well . . .

JANE

You don't think we've fooled anyone, do you?

PHILIP

I do indeed.

JANE

Everyone in the hotel knows.

PHILIP

That's not true. How?

JANE

The elevator operators.

PHILIP

I've been using the stairs!

JANE

Have you, really?

PHILIP

Don't start admiring me again. It's only one flight. I'll have to ask you to be seated.

JANE

Why?

PHILIP

Just do as I say. (*She does. He fishes in his pocket for the box*) Now. I have in this box a token of my esteem and regard.

JANE

You've given me quite enough presents.

PHILIP

I like to give you presents. This box is not to be opened until tomorrow night, at midnight.

JANE

I'd like to ask you something. Did you give your wife as many presents, before you were separated?

PHILIP

(*Displeased*) This isn't much of a subject.

JANE

I'm very curious.

PHILIP

(*Still displeased*) Well, I guess so. Why do you ask?

JANE

I'm trying to figure out whether you're truly generous, or it's your conscience. Many people get credit for doing admirable things that they really do because they'd be uncomfortable if they didn't.

PHILIP

I hope that's from a play you were in, because it's damn silly.

JANE

It's from the play I'm in now.

PHILIP

I don't remember that. (*He tries again*) Now about this present—

JANE

It looks very expensive. It's so small.

PHILIP

(*Impatient*) Yes, it is expensive—

JANE

Well, I'll take it. I've earned it.

PHILIP

Jane! What's gotten into you tonight!

JANE

You've had the best years of my life!

PHILIP

You're acting strangely. You've been in a dozen different moods, most of which I've never seen before.

JANE

Mystery, that's my stock in trade. I'm a woman, you know.

PHILIP

I know. I'll testify to that. Now will you get in another mood? Less flippant, please. I'll wait.

JANE

What would you like?

PHILIP

Nothing makes a man feel more ridiculous than being sentimental while the woman is not. I have an elaborate scheme that goes with this present.

JANE

You want sentiment, eh? (*She looks at the box he's holding*)
You're sure it's expensive? Well, I can do that, I'm an actress.

PHILIP

You couldn't deceive me.

JANE

(*Hard*) You'd be surprised.

PHILIP

I'm waiting for the new mood. (*She's going to do it*)

JANE

Darling, I'm going to miss you terribly. I'll walk into a crowded
room and someone will be standing the way you stand. He'll
hold his head the way you hold your head. The way you hold
your knife and fork—

PHILIP

I don't hold my knife and fork any special way.

JANE

Why, you hold your fork straight up, as a little boy does.

PHILIP

That speech is from your play! Hmm. How often have you
used dialogue from plays you've been in?

JANE

I don't know myself. I start a sentence on my own but halfway
through it seems familiar to me. I just don't think about it
any more.

PHILIP

I've been making love to a dozen authors.

JANE

More.

PHILIP

Still, some of your material must have been original. I can't
picture the situation on the stage.

JANE

I've been in all kinds of plays.

PHILIP

Still—

JANE

Life follows art. There isn't a situation in life that hasn't its
formula in the theatre. Including the one we're in now.

PHILIP

(*Puzzled*) You are in a strange mood. Kind of deep. (*He de-
cides on a new strategy. He places the box on the coffee table.
He puts his arms around her and kisses her. At first she's pas-
sive, then she puts her arms around him, returning the kiss.
It's not impulsive on her part. They break*) What part are
you playing now?

JANE

Delilah.

PHILIP

From the Bible? I don't see the parallel.

JANE

It's my own interpretation.

PHILIP

Well, as long as I'm going to be destroyed anyway— (*He would kiss her again, but the phone rings*) For heaven's sake! It's going to be that kind of an evening! (*Jane goes to the phone*)

JANE

It's only Margaret.

PHILIP

How that woman loves to telephone! What would she have done a hundred years ago?

JANE

(*Into phone*) Hello. . . . (*Her hand over phone, to keep his voice out*) Ssh!

PHILIP

Probably sent carrier pigeons! The sky'd've been black!

JANE

(*Into phone*) Why, hello David! This is quite a surprise! (*Philip is rigid, formal. She looks to him. He pantomimes, courteously, that he will leave, and starts. Jane has her hand over the phone*) Don't you dare leave!

PHILIP

You may wish to speak privately.

JANE

(*Hand still over phone*) Aren't you cured of that childish jealousy?

PHILIP

It's not jealousy, it's common courtesy.

JANE

Well, you're starting to turn beet red again! (*Into phone having to answer immediately*) No, I'm not alone. Annie's here.
. . . . (*Philip turns quickly, unable to stay*)

PHILIP

Annie's leaving! (*He strides to the guest bedroom door*)

JANE

(*Into phone*) Annie's just leaving. (*Philip slams the inner door, loud. Jane smiles in satisfaction*) I'm not interested in Alfred's advice. . . . Let Alfred take a sleeping pill. . . . Good night. (*She hangs up. She looks to the door, grimly pleased at the testing. She goes to the bar, takes a quick drink, straight, and then to the guest bedroom door, calling*) You can come out now. (*He does. He has decided to appear calm*)

PHILIP

Although it may be hard for you to believe, I have quite overcome my old, ridiculous trait of jealousy.

JANE

Have you?

PHILIP

Yes, I have. And I have you thank for it.

JANE

I'm so glad. I was so afraid when you left the room just now you were displeased.

PHILIP

I was displeased. That's not the same as jealousy. I'm a very honest man. I am displeased at his calling you.

JANE

(*Meaningly*) Yes, you are honest. I'm going to match your honesty.

PHILIP

What do you mean? (*She goes to her purse and opens it. Her back is to him and his curiosity brings him to looking over her shoulder*)

JANE

I've been hiding this from you.

PHILIP

What is it?

JANE

(*Popping it out*) It's a *red* rose. (*The sudden appearance of the flower in his face gives him a start*)

PHILIP

David! (*She nods, sadly*) Where did you get it? Where did it come from?

JANE

I didn't have confidence in you. I wasn't going to let you know about it. I'm ashamed of myself.

PHILIP

Did he give it to you this evening? Where? (*He doesn't let her answer*) Was he at El Morocco? (*She nods again*) Was there a note with it? (*She shakes her head*) Did he bring it over himself?

JANE

A waiter brought it over.

PHILIP

(*Oblivious to the impression he's making*) Then he didn't speak to you?

JANE

He did.

PHILIP

(*District attorney*) When? How? I danced with you all evening! I was with you every minute!

JANE

When I went to the powder room. He followed me out.

PHILIP

(*It takes him a moment to compose his face*) I will not descend to commenting on him, I will merely say this hardly flatters you. I pictured more of a—gentleman.

JANE

David's a gentleman. Take my word for it.

PHILIP

Oh, come now.

JANE

You'd like him. Yes, you would. You two would get along fine.

PHILIP

Hardly. I don't consider myself a snob, but I am sure there is no one among my acquaintances who follows women to powder rooms!

JANE

I may be doing him a disservice. He may not have been following me at all. It might have just been coincidence.

PHILIP

No, he was following you!

JANE

In any case, have I done the right thing in telling you?

PHILIP

Certainly you have!

JANE

You're not upset?

PHILIP

Not in the slightest! I'm pleased!

JANE

Pleased!

PHILIP

Frankly, I was always curious of the measure of the man! I'm not any more.

JANE

I'm glad. That's the right way to look at it.

PHILIP

What did he say on the phone?

JANE

(*She needs a moment*) On the phone?

PHILIP

I'm sorry, I wasn't asking. You were explaining about him and I thought you meant to tell me. I was just helping the conversation along.

JANE

I don't mind telling you.

PHILIP

I'd rather not hear it.

JANE

But I'd like to tell you.

PHILIP

It's of no interest to me whatsoever.

JANE

He asked me to go out with him.

PHILIP

What did you say?

JANE

Here or at El Morocco?

PHILIP

He asked you at both places?

JANE

Well, he asked me there, and I said 'no.' And he just asked me again.

PHILIP

And what did you say?

JANE

What do you think I said? Absolutely not. (*There is a moment*)

PHILIP

If you feel like it, why don't you go out with him? You're old friends.

JANE

Oh, Philip! You're truly cured! I liked you better when you were jealous!

PHILIP

(*Generous in victory*) No, I mean it! You'll be lonely the next two weeks. I wouldn't mind.

JANE

(*She looks at him adoringly, he thinks*) I couldn't. I couldn't! (*She puts her arms around him, her head on his shoulder*) The thing I like about you, darling, is you're so fair.

PHILIP

I think I am. (*They kiss*) I try to be very objective. Now sending a rose to a table, that's really adolescent.

JANE

Well . .

PHILIP

And he's not very considerate, calling you at this hour.

JANE

He knows I don't go to bed until later. (*Philip bristles*) I'm sorry! That was the wrong thing to have said! Try to forget it! Put it out of your mind!

PHILIP

From an evening that started well, this has turned into one of the most exasperating evenings of my whole life!

JANE

(*For herself*) Your life isn't over yet.

PHILIP

I think any ex-suitor who doesn't realize he's an ex-suitor—
and doesn't stay ex—is the most despicable kind of human
being, and I'd say it to his face!

JANE

He's taller than you.

PHILIP

That did it! I'm leaving!

JANE

Good night, dear.

PHILIP

Good night, my foot! (*He takes her in his arms again, kissing
her*) Sweetheart . . .

JANE

(*In his arms*) Darling— (*It looks as though they mean it. They
keep at it quite a while*)

PHILIP

(*Tenderly*) What is it?

JANE

I've a splitting headache. (*Philip releases her instantly*) Don't
be irritated now. It's only your vanity.

PHILIP

I'm not irritated at all.

JANE

Yes, you are. If a man and woman don't fuse together the
same moment the man is always hurt. That's from 'Private
Lives.' I played it on the road.

PHILIP

For heaven's sake, I've been kissing Noel Coward!

JANE

You could do worse. A few minutes ago it was Ibsen. Darling, don't be mean. You're leaving tomorrow!

PHILIP

I wish I'd left yesterday!

JANE

I can't help the headache. That's why I've been acting strangely. I've been trying to hide it.

PHILIP

(*All contrite*) I'm awfully sorry. I'm not behaving too well.

JANE

Yes you are. Considering you're worried whether I've gotten the splitting headache only since the phone call. (*He says nothing*) Aren't you? Aren't you?

PHILIP

(*Smiling*) No more.

JANE

(*She holds her arms out. He moves in*) You are transparent. (*Her expression becomes ironic, which he cannot see*) And I'm so clever.

PHILIP

Remember. When you hear the chimes—

JANE

I'll raise my glass.

PHILIP

Be sure now.

JANE

I will.

PHILIP

I'd feel foolish drinking by myself, out at sea.

JANE

How would you know?

PHILIP

Intuition. Men have it, too.

JANE

Good night, darling. (*She gives him a big kiss*)

PHILIP

Good night, sweet.

JANE

Take care.

PHILIP

I will. Act good.

JANE

And write.

PHILIP

I'll phone. Goodbye, my darling. (*A kiss on the cheek. He walks to the exit, Rear. She stands where she is. He turns, framed in the arch*) I've seen plays with wonderful 'goodbye' lines in them, I'm trying to remember one.

JANE

I've heard them all.

PHILIP

I guess you have. Oh well, goodbye.

JANE

Very clever. And to the point.

PHILIP

Don't forget. Tomorrow at midnight!

JANE

I'm thinking about it right now.

CURTAIN

ACT THREE

Scene Two

It is shortly before midnight, the following evening. The room is filled with red roses. A table is fixed for supper for two, Center, Right. The gift-wrapped box that Philip gave Jane is on the table. There is also a pot of coffee.

Annie enters from pantry, carrying the copper casserole for supper. She places it on its stand on the table. She lights a match, and the spirit lamp under the casserole. She surveys the table.

Jane, in a boudoir robe, enters from her bedroom. She, too, surveys the table. She looks around, goes to a small vase of red roses, and brings them to the supper table, grimly pleased. She looks about.

JANE

Do you think we've overdone the flowers?

ANNIE

(*Uncertainly*) We've never had this many before.

JANE

How many are there?

ANNIE

You told me to get three dozen, and then the box came from Mister Wilson with two dozen. That's five dozen altogether.

JANE

It is a little thick. (*Fans herself*) Smells like a flower show.

ANNIE

Shall I take some out?

JANE

(*Thinking*) No, they have to be noticeable. They have to stick out! I want them to be seen at first glance! Leave them!

ANNIE

Yes mam. (*Jane looks toward the table*) Chicken a la king, and I took the champagne out of the ice-box, so it's cold.

JANE

(*Looking at her watch*) Very good, Annie. (*She's concerned. She goes to the phone, Annie leaves through pantry door. Into phone*) Molly, what time have you? (*Evidently it is as late as Jane fears*) Would you call Eldorado 6-3131? (*She waits, another look at her watch*) Mister Wilson, please. David Wilson. . . . Thank you, no message. Could you tell me how long ago he left? . . . (*Disappointment*) Did *he* leave any message? . . . He didn't. . . . Thank you very much. . . . (*She hangs up, concerned, and the phone rings while she has her hand on it. Eagerly*) Hello? . . . Yes! . . . Who? . . . Yes! . . . Oh no! . . . Oh no! . . . (*Flat*) Yes, Doctor! Remember me to him. . . . Tell him he has my sympathy . . . Thank you, Doctor. (*She hangs up. Deep despair. Her chin cupped in her hand. Annie enters from pantry, carrying water glasses on a tray. She places the glasses on the table, noticing Jane's behavior*)

ANNIE

Excuse me. Is something the matter?

JANE

They carried Mister Wilson off the handball court of the New York Athletic Club at five o'clock this afternoon with acute appendicitis!

ANNIE

Oh, my!

JANE

He was on the operating table forty-five minutes. The operaton was very successful.

ANNIE

I'm glad.

JANE

The first thing he said when he came out of the ether was, "Call Miss Kimball and apologize for me."

ANNIE

Wasn't that considerate!

JANE

Considerate! What the hell was he doing playing handball! (*Annie doesn't know what to say. She looks to the supper*)

ANNIE

Would you like some chicken a la king?

JANE

No!

ANNIE

It'll make you feel better.

JANE

No, it won't!

ANNIE

You haven't had anything to eat since before the show. I'll give you just a little.

JANE

I don't want any chicken a la king!

ANNIE

Yes mam.

JANE

I want a man! I need a man, tonight! Now! Right now!

ANNIE

A man? Do you want to lift something? Carl's here.

JANE

Carl?

ANNIE

Carl's not very big, but he's strong. You'd be surprised.

JANE

Carl?

ANNIE

Shall I ask him to come in?

JANE

Yes. We'll audition him. (*She gets up, thinking, as Annie goes to pantry door*)

ANNIE

(*Calling*) Carl! Come in here! (*Carl enters from pantry, always shy in front of Jane*)

CARL

Good evening, Miss Kimball.

JANE

(*Looking him over carefully*) Hello, Carl. How are you?

CARL

I'm fine, thank you.

ANNIE

(*Apprehensive about Jane's scrutiny*) What do you want him for?

JANE

Of course he knows you. Still—. Put the wall lights out, Annie. (*Annie does. The remaining lamps make a more obscure Carl*) It would only be for a few seconds. Walk around, Carl. (*Indicating the area near the master bedroom door, which is the darkest*) Over there. (*He just stands there, lost*)

ANNIE

Walk! (*He walks*)

CARL

(*Walking*) Where?

ANNIE

Up and down. Can't you just walk? (*He walks. Jane thinks. Annie looks to her*)

JANE

Annie, bring me Mister Clair's dressing gown. (*Annie goes to the guest bedroom*)

JANE

You can stop walking, Carl. (*He stops*) Take off your glasses. (*She surveys him again*) It's dark enough. (*Carl has been trying to put his glasses on the table, but has missed the table*) Don't you see well without your glasses?

CARL

(*Looking to her left by ten feet*) Not small things.

JANE

You better put them on again. (*He does. Annie comes back with the robe*) Give it to him. (*Annie helps Carl on with it. It's too big*)

CARL

(*Dangling the sleeves*) They're a little long, but I could shorten them.

ANNIE

Walk some more! (*He does*)

JANE

His own dressing gown! It's a good touch! (*She's made up her mind to use him*) Carl, I'm thinking of playing a practical joke on a friend of mine. I wonder if you'd care to help me.

ANNIE

Certainly he will!

CARL

A practical joke? Will anyone be hurt?

JANE

Not physically—

ANNIE

It's none of your business.

CARL

I only asked. As long as I'm the one—

ANNIE

What do you want him to do?

JANE

At exactly midnight I'd like you to open that door, let Mister
Clair see you for just one second, and jump back into the room,
closing the door behind you.

CARL

(*It's becoming clear to him*) Mister Clair'll be here?

JANE

That's who we're playing the joke on.

CARL

(*He's had enough*) I wouldn't want to spoil it for you. (*He
starts to take the robe off*) I don't think I could do it good.
You should have an actor, not a tailor.

ANNIE

I thought you were a wardrobe man.

CARL

It turns out I'm a tailor.

JANE

There'll be no danger, if that's your concern.

CARL

I've seen a lot of plays in my time. Jealous lovers, excuse me,
they either have a gun or a knife, or a poker from the fireplace
—anyway, somebody's always lying on the floor.

ANNIE

Carl, you're a coward.

CARL

(*Nodding*) That's true. All my life I've been a coward.

ANNIE

You ought to be ashamed of yourself.

CARL

I'm ashamed.

JANE

Mister Clair won't harm you. You can lock the door behind you.

ANNIE

And you can hide under the bed! (*Carl looks at Annie a moment, and puts the robe on again*)

CARL

Why am I wasting everybody's time?

JANE

Thank you, Carl.

CARL

But I'm going to lock the door! What do you want me to do?

JANE

All you have to do is listen for the chimes, and come out on the twelfth chime. Just step out, one step, that'll be enough, and then step back and close the door.

CARL

And lock it!

JANE

Yes, you can lock it. The important thing is to count with the chimes and come out exactly on the last one.

CARL

Maybe we should have a rehearsal?

ANNIE

What's the matter, can't you count to twelve?

CARL

I can count fine! But the stepping out and the stepping back, it has to be right!

ANNIE

Look, he's giving a performance! Why, you big ham—

JANE

Just a moment! We need a rehearsal. You get in there, and listen for the chimes. Annie'll be the chimes. Come out on the twelfth chime.

CARL

(*Dignity now, having thrown a look of satisfaction to Annie*) Very well. Twelfth chime. That's my cue. (*He exits to master bedroom, Right, closing the door behind him. There is a loud click as the lock is turned*)

ANNIE

My hero! (*Jane goes to the table for two, and sits. Annie goes to the master bedroom door*) Ready?

JANE

Begin!

ANNIE

Bong! (*She will 'Bong' soft enough not to interfere with Jane's performance*)

JANE

Philip! (*She stands up. She combines acting out her part, and indicating what Philip will do*) What are you doing here? He'll stand there, disappointed I'm not drinking a toast to him. It'll take him a moment to understand what he sees. Supper for two. Then the red roses. Then he'll look back to me. I'll look toward the door. Frightened. I'll walk toward it— (*She does*)—putting it between us. Speechless. Hand to my mouth. (*Annie has gotten to the twelfth 'BONG'. The master bedroom door opens and Carl steps out and back, real good, slamming it behind him. We hear the lock click. Jane lets her hand fall. Then raises it*) What can I say? I'm sorry you had to find out. I'm sorry it had to end this way. (*She takes the box from the table, tears the wrapping off, opens it, and dangles a magnificent bracelet from her two fingers*) It's a beautiful bracelet. I hope you can return it. (*She holds it out. Annie is pop-eyed*)

ANNIE

Are—those—emeralds? (*Jane nods grimly*)

JANE

That's what they are!

ANNIE

They come that size?

JANE

These do! One thing you can't call him, is cheap. But you can call him everything else!

ANNIE

(*Hopefully*) Maybe he won't take it?

JANE

I was in a play once where I gave a present back. The man refused to take it, he threw it at me. It was a cameo brooch.

ANNIE

Cameo brooches they throw, not emeralds! Are you sure you still want to do this?

JANE

I'm sure! Go on! (*Puts bracelet on table. Carl comes out of the master bedroom*)

CARL

How was I?

ANNIE

You'll steal all the notices.

JANE

You were fine, Carl. (*She looks at her watch*) Pretty soon! (*A few steps*) Put the food on the plates! Carl, go back in the room! And do it just the way you did it! (*Annie will ladle the chicken a la king out of the chafing dish onto the plates*)

CARL

I'm a little bit nervous.

ANNIE

Well, stop it! Go on! (*He exits into the master bedroom*)

ANNIE

(*Pouring*) And the coffee. I once worked for Belasco. All the props had to be real.

JANE

(*At her watch*) All right, Annie.

ANNIE

I'll be listening. (*Annie exits into guest room. Jane seats herself, carefully. She looks at her watch. She waits. We hear her softly repeating her lines*)

JANE

(*A mumble*) Philip! What are you doing here? What can I say? I'm sorry—(*The rest silent lip movement. We hear the first chime, and with it, the outer door opening. Philip appears*) Philip! (*She stands up*) What are you doing here? (*Philip comes into the room, his eyes glued to her, oblivious to the supper for two and the red roses*)

PHILIP

My darling! Something enormous has happened! I've just had word my wife died! She was an invalid so long it was a blessing! Do you hear me, darling? We can be married! (*He takes her in his arms. We are now up to the twelfth 'Bong.' The master bedroom door flies open, Carl steps out, directly in his line of vision, and steps back. The door slams. Philip slowly releases her. Jane watches all this as in a dream. Philip looks from her to the supper for two. And then the red roses. As in a trance, Jane takes the bracelet from the table*)

JANE

(*Not the rehearsed reading. A machine*) What can I say? I'm sorry you had to find out. I'm sorry it had to end this way. (*She holds the bracelet out*) It's a beautiful bracelet. I hope you can return it. (*She is almost in tears. Philip looks at the door, at her, at the bracelet. He is in a stupor of his own. He takes the bracelet. He turns slowly and goes out hall door. We hear the door close after him. Jane goes to the couch and sits. Annie comes out, Left*)

ANNIE

(*Agonized*) Oh, Miss Kimball!

JANE

(*In a trance*) There was nothing I could do! Nothing! There was nothing anybody could do! (*Carl comes out, from master bedroom, slowly, first seeing if the coast is clear. They watch him*)

CARL

(*High*) How was I?

ANNIE

Shut up, you old fool! (*Carl is puzzled*) Maybe if you told him the truth, Miss Kimball?

JANE

(*Calm*) No. This is the way it was meant to be. It's fate! Kismet

CARL

(*Bewildered*) Did I spoil something?

JANE

Not you, Carl. Me. I did it. With my little hatchet.

ANNIE

I can go to him and explain the whole thing. He'll believe me.

CARL

Did something go wrong?

JANE

Nothing much. A small thing. My life. That's all.

ANNIE

Oh, Miss Kimball! (*The outer door is heard bursting open, and slams. Carl becomes rigid, and then dashes for his haven Right, senses he can't make it, and ducks behind the piano for concealment. He is just in time, but he loses his glasses. Philip has come to, and he's in a restrained rage*)

PHILIP

This bracelet wasn't a gift! It was payment! For what you earned! We were on a cash basis! (*And he tosses the bracelet on the plate. He thinks he is looking triumphant*) And where is my rival? (*He assumes he is in the bedroom still*) I'm afraid I may have seemed rude to him! He has my apology! I'm in his debt! (*He goes into the master bedroom. Carl now rises from under the piano and gropes for the door, but without his glasses cannot find the direction. He paws the drapes. Annie signals from across the room, but it is no use. Philip re-enters, and Carl dives back*) I can think of no man to whom I'm more indebted! (*Philip crosses to the opposite bedroom at Left*) Is he here? (*Annie, standing in front of the opposite bedroom, shakes her head, and indicates the open door leading out of the apartment. This satisfies him*) When I think that I actually proposed marriage! Marriage! I'll never be intolerant of another fool as long as I live! Would you like to hear a further insanity? At three o'clock this morning, walking up and down my living room, searching my soul, I questioned whether I was worthy of you! Worthy of you! I took a vow—and not in the bathroom!—that I would never let one suspicion of jealousy ever enter my mind again, because to be jealous of any conduct of yours would be—and this is the word I used—would be—sacrilege! (*Unbelieving*) Sacrilege! (*Carl gropes for his glasses, and suddenly Philip becomes conscious of the movement. He peers, puzzled. He strides to the wall switch, and flicks it on. Jane runs to Annie's arms. They cling to each other*)

PHILIP

This does not become you, my friend! And you are my friend! (*No movement*) Stand up, man, I haven't a gun! I said, 'Stand up'! (*He looks to Jane, in contempt at what she has chosen*) You're straining our friendship, stand up! (*Philip bends down to see better*) That's—my—dressing gown you're wearing! You've gone a little too far! Take it off! Right now! (*He starts to unbutton his coat*) There is also the insult of following a lady I am with—*any* lady I am with—to the powder room! I do not like a sneak! I will count to three! One—two—(*The coat is off, when Carl appears*)

CARL

They made me do it!

PHILIP

Carl!

CARL

I don't know anything!

PHILIP

Do you mean—! (*He indicates the master bedroom, and then Carl. It slowly sinks in*)

JANE

You're not married! You're dishonest! (*Philip just stands, deflated. Annie reaches for the plate bearing the bracelet and offers it, two fingers holding the bracelet, to Philip. He ignores her. Annie looks to Carl. Carl signals for her to get away. Annie puts the plate down, Carl takes her by the arm and huries her off, Rear, Right*)

PHILIP

(*Finally*) You shouldn't have done it. It was a cheap and shoddy thing to do.

JANE

I didn't start being cheap and shoddy.

PHILIP

(*He shakes his head*) It didn't become you. It didn't become our relationship.

JANE

What was our relationship, may I ask?

PHILIP

(*Strong*) It was something fine and spiritual! That's what it was!

JANE

On whose part? On mine! I contributed the fine and spiritual! You lied and cheated!

PHILIP

I was honorable! I stuck to the rules!

JANE

The rules! You're not going to bring up the rules again?

PHILIP

Yes I am! What can man go by but rules? I was honorable! And sensible! You weren't! When you found out I wasn't married you shouldn't have done anything about it. You should have kept it from me! That's what a clever woman would have done!

JANE

Kept it from you!

PHILIP

Yes! I'd've come 'round to marrying you! You notice I did!

JANE

(*Calm, reflective*) But you wouldn't have, if I hadn't made you jealous. Not in a thousand years.

PHILIP

Nonsense, I might have proposed a little later, but it was inevitable.

JANE

Not true. What's inevitable is we were fated not to be married. There was a chance for a moment, but we lost it. It's too bad, too, because I love you very much and we could have been quite happy.

PHILIP

We can still be happy.

JANE

Maybe. Lord knows any happiness is difficult enough to find. (*A moment*) It's not too becoming from a woman, but we're hardly strangers—and knowing your passion for rules—I'll make the proposition. If you're willing, I'm willing. The last two days never happened.

PHILIP

What do you mean?

JANE

I mean we'll go on as before.

PHILIP

And not be married?

JANE

That's right.

PHILIP

(*A moment*) That's the most indecent thing I ever heard of!

JANE

What?

PHILIP

I can't believe my ears!

JANE

What are you so shocked about?

PHILIP

I didn't think you were capable of it!

JANE

What's different?

PHILIP

We're not married!

JANE

We weren't before!

PHILIP

You didn't *know* I wasn't married!

JANE

You knew!

PHILIP

I knew *you* didn't know! (*Jane looks at him with great love and understanding*) What's the matter with you? How could you ask me to do such a thing? Haven't you been following what I've been saying? (*She starts to sniffle*) I tell you women are not the sensitive sex! It's one of the great delusions of literature! Men are the true romanticists. I tell you—What are you crying about?

JANE

(*Tenderly*) Oh, shut up! (*He takes her in his arms*)

PHILIP

Don't cry, Jane. I love you. Everything'll be all right. You'll like being married. You'll see, you will. There, darling. There, darling. (*He gives her his handkerchief. She pushes it aside and hugs him, laughing and crying*)

JANE

Oh, Philp! Philip!

CURTAIN

PROPERTY LIST

On Stage

D.R.C.: Brass table and 3 chairs

Cigarettes and paper of matches in crystal box on table

D.R. Piano and stool

On piano: Sheet music; large brass flower holding stand; 2 candle sticks

R. of upper end of piano: Pedestal holding large lamp

R. rear wall: desk and chair

L. " " : sideboard with: 2 lamps; water in glass pitcher; seltzer bottle; large silver tray with: bottles of brandy, scotch, vodka, 3 highball glasses, 2 shot glasses; ice in ice bucket. (liquor, glasses, inside cab.)

On platform U.C.: Large secretary; statuette

Below L. doorway: magazine rack with: "Ill. London News," "Ladies Home Journal," "New Yorker," "Town and Country," "N.Y. Herald-Tribune"

On mantel piece: 3 vases with flowers; hand mirror

In fireplace: Fire screen, andirons, logs

D.L. straight chair

L.C. Large sofa with 2 bolsters

Below sofa: large coffee table practical for sitting on

Above sofa: long table with: telephone at R. end, 3 ash trays, "New Yorker," paper of matches

L. of sofa: Arm chair

L. of arm chair: sewing table with sewing bag, needle point in work, Jane's glasses

By sewing table, special sewing lamp

Carpet; draperies

Act I, Scene 1

Off *U.R.C.*: Play script and four or five unopened letters (Annie)

Off *U.L.C.*: Tan cowhide suitcase (Alfred's); alligator suitcase (Philip)

Act I, Scene 2

> *Off U.R.C.*: Sewing basket with: wrist pin cushion with pins and (threaded needle for Carl), tape measure, needles, thread; (Annie), Yard stick (Annie); Skirt (Annie); Silent Butler with dust cloth (Annie); Ice in ice bucket (Annie)

Act II, Scene 1

> *Off R.*: (Master bedroom): Ring in wrapped box (Philip)
> *Off U.R.C.*: Play script, inserted page of "rehearsal" (Annie)

Act II, Scene 2

> *On table D.R.C.*: sheaf of bills; bills on spindle; pencils; ash tray
> *On piano*: Book for Alfred to slam
> *Off U.L.C.*: Cowhide bag (Alfred); Brief case (Philip); Dress box (Jane)

Act III, Scene 1

> *Off U.R.C.*: Cup of tea (Annie)
> *Off U.L.C.*: Bracelet in wrapped box (Philip); red rose in Jane's handbag (personal prop)

Act III, Scene 2

> *Off U.R.C.*: 2 vases red roses for mantel (Carl) tall vase red roses (Carl) 2 bowls red roses (Carl) Tray with: chafing dish, large spoon, large plate, coffee pot, 2 demi-tasse spoons, 2 demi-tasse cups & saucers; 2 highball glasses. (Set by props.) Folded table cloth, 2 knives and forks, 2 spoons, prompt paper reading: "I'm sorry you had to find out. I'm sorry it had to end this way. It's a beautiful bracelet; I hope you can return it.", garland of red roses. (Annie)
> *Off U.R.*: (Jane's room) Basket of red roses (Jane) Candelabra (set by props on desk)

Plot for flowers

I-1: Mantel: 2 vases; 1 bowl (fall flowers); Piano: lilies

I-2: same

II-1: Piano: yellow roses; sofa tables: bowl of yellow roses; desk: bowl of yellow roses; off D.R.: Basket of yellow roses

II-2: Piano: spring flowers; Desk: spring flowers; Sofa table: same as I-3; Strike flowers from mantel and replace with yellow roses from desk

III-1: same

III-2: Piano: red roses; sofa table, red roses; desk: red roses; mantel: red roses. Garland on arm of statuette

Personal props

    Jane: red rose in handbag for III-1, dress box
    Margaret: door key, gloves, small overnight suitcase
    Philip: Glasses, notebook, door key, watch, handkerchief, cigarette case
    Alfred: watch, cigarettes, matches
    Carl: Glasses, watch
    Annie: Lists of paper

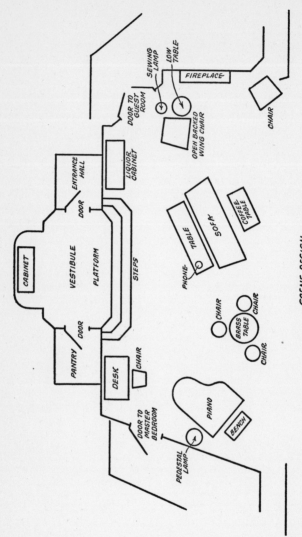

SCENE DESIGN
"KIND SIR"